Praise for *The Stream*

In *The Stream*, James Robison helps us to recognize the extreme value of freedom and why we must fight for it every day through our Christian witness. The Declaration of Independence indicates that our rights come from God, and this important book points out many ways that we can use our lives to preserve those freedoms and reconnect with the founding principles that made America great.

—Benjamin S. Carson Sr., MD
Emeritus Professor of Neurosurgery, Oncology, Plastic Surgery and Pediatrics
Johns Hopkins Medicine
President and CEO, American Business Collaborative, LLC

Over thirty-five years ago God used James Robison to ignite a nation for the purpose of returning back to our Judeo-Christian heritage. His Bible-based leadership mobilized Christians to participate in prophetic activism for the purpose of sharing truth with love. Once again, God calls upon James Robison, and via *The Stream*, he equips us with the Christ-centered, Bible-based prescription for these troubled times.

—Rev. Dr. Samuel Rodriguez
President, NHCLC/CONELA Hispanic Evangelical Association

Pastor Robison is a religious patriot—a spokesman whose love for America is rooted in the religious beliefs embodied in America's history. In *The Stream* he sets forth his noble vision of how a nation guided by the Almighty will find blessing and harmony. Toward that end, he urges people of The Book to involve themselves in our country's political destiny and bring forth a land reflective of their traditional values. Read it and be uplifted . . . and called.

—Rabbi Aryeh Spero
President, Caucus for America

In *The Stream*, my friend James Robison provides us with a reliable roadmap out of the darkness of dissention and into the glorious light that only wisdom from above can provide. America can once again be a beacon of hope, but to do so, we need to act on this wisdom now.

—Gretchen Carlson
Award-winning host of *The Real Story with Gretchen Carlson*, FOX News
Author of the best-selling book *Getting Real*

Few have stood for truth and righteousness more than James Robison. This living legend has never been intimidated by the threats of Satan or the dangerous currents in our culture. Read *The Stream* and hear his courageous voice to our nation, which is filled with compassion overflowing.

—Dr. Ronnie Floyd

President, Southern Baptist Convention

Senior Pastor, Cross Church, Springdale, AR

Once, we were a nation under God, indivisible, with liberty for all. Now we are on the verge of becoming a nation under many gods—or no God—divisible, with liberty for none. James Robison intends to see that that doesn't happen—not without a clarion call to repentance and revival. If ever there was a message needed for America today, this is it!

—Dr. Robert Jeffress

Senior Pastor, First Baptist Church of Dallas

As a talk show host, I hear arguments and sharp opinions all the time. It is always refreshing to hear James Robison's take on the blessings of liberty. He is always ready to do battle for freedom, but in a compassionate and welcoming way that we need in these tense times.

—Mark Davis

Host of *The Mark Davis Show* radio broadcast

James Robison offers a shining light of hope as a sharp contrast to his honest look at our current state of affairs in America. If the church can grasp the incredible opportunity we have at this moment in history, as James suggests—we have the potential to see the world's greatest ever awakening.

—Christine Caine

Founder A21 and Propel Women

In his new book, *The Stream*, my friend and mentor James Robison encourages you to get out of your comfort zone and fulfill the Great Commission. I believe, if we as believers step out and do this, we will see our nation's foundation restored. I hope all those who cherish their freedom will read this book and hear the truth straight from God's heart.

—Robert Morris

Founding Senior Pastor, Gateway Church, Southlake, TX

The Stream drills deep into the refreshing stream of life-giving water that must flow freely if we are to rise up as the church and see the heart of America restored.

—Sheila Walsh
Author, speaker, and Christian recording artist

My good friend James Robison has given us an insightful, inspirational, yet sober and challenging message for all who wish to see our beloved republic return from the principles of destruction and despair to become the beacon of light that it could be. The message of *The Stream* is critical for all who wish to understand our spiritual crisis and who desire to be a part of seeing it reversed.

—Tony Evans
President, The Urban Alternative
Senior Pastor, Oak Cliff Bible Fellowship

James Robison is a world-renowned Christian thought leader respected across the denominational spectrum. In *The Stream*, he lays out a clear analysis of where we are as a nation and gives us a road map to claiming our collective, national inheritance. Jesus is confronting sacred cows, exposing hypocrisy, and turning tables right side up in our day. This is why *The Stream* is a must-read for everyone from the pulpit to the pew. A must-read for everyone who longs for a revival of righteousness and a spiritual awakening in America. Every page of this book is dripping with the wisdom of God and is grounded in authenticity. *The Stream* refreshes the weary soul.

—Bishop Harry Jackson
Senior Pastor, Hope Christian Church, Beltsville, MD
Founder and Chairman, High Impact Leadership Coalition

James Robison and I share the same heartfelt concerns for our nation. The First Amendment is under attack, and freedom to express and live out our religious convictions is under a fierce assault. What James provides in this excellent work inspires and equips Christians to have a salt-and-light effect on the culture around us. You will be challenged to take a bold stand to help secure our nation's freedom and security.

—Mat Staver
Founder and Chairman, Liberty Counsel
Founder and President, Covenant Journey

As a pastor, I understand the significance of being involved and trying to awaken, enlighten, and activate Christians so we can impact our culture. This is releasing the imprint of the kingdom of God on earth. James Robison will inspire you to become ambassadors for Christ—releasing streams of love and transforming necessary to protect and preserve our precious freedoms.

—Dr. Jim Garlow
Pastor, Skyline Church, San Diego, CA

Writing with passion, love, and truth, James Robison brings an urgent warning to America. It is not too late for the nation, but the clock is ticking, and we must respond with urgency and faith. Relying on the truths of Scripture and the lessons of history, James shows us how we must live to see America transformed. It is now or never. How will we respond?

—Dr. Michael L. Brown
Host, *Line of Fire* radio broadcast
President, FIRE School of Ministry

James Robison serves as a father figure to countless church leaders—including us. We value his commitment to awaken America and the church from deep slumber. The biblical wisdom, inspiration, and history he packs into this book will give you hope and encourage you to pray fervently for this great nation.

—John and Lisa Bevere
Founders, Messenger International

There is a war on traditional values in America—and our general in this battle is James Robison. He understands that we cannot win this fight in the state house. It must be won in the church house—through lives changed by the saving grace of Jesus. James Robison's new book is must-reading for every Bible-believing patriot in America. I'm reading my copy right now—in my fox hole on the front lines of the culture war.

—Todd Starnes
FOX News Channel

JAMES ROBISON

THE
STREAM

REFRESHING HEARTS & MINDS
RENEWING FREEDOM'S BLESSINGS

WORTHY®
PUBLISHING

Published by Worthy Books, an imprint of Worthy Publishing Group, a division of Worthy Media, Inc., One Franklin Park, 6100 Tower Circle, Suite 210, Franklin, TN 37067.

WORTHY is a registered trademark of Worthy Media, Inc.

HELPING PEOPLE EXPERIENCE THE HEART OF GOD

eBook available wherever digital books are sold.

Library of Congress Cataloging-in-Publication Data

Names: Robison, James, 1943- author.
Title: The stream : restoring life to our parched nation / James Robison.
Description: Franklin, TN : Worthy Publishing, 2016.
Identifiers: LCCN 2016011304 | ISBN 9781617957581 (hardcover)
Subjects: LCSH: Christianity--United States. | United States--Church history.
| United States--Moral conditions.
Classification: LCC BR515 .R5535 2016 | DDC 261.0973--dc23
LC record available at http://lccn.loc.gov/2016011304

For foreign and subsidiary rights, contact rights@worthypublishing.com

ISBN: 978-1-61795-758-1

Cover Design: Matt Smartt/ Smartt Guys design
Interior Design and Typesetting: Bart Dawson

Printed in the United States of America
16 17 18 19 20 BVG 8 7 6 5 4 3 2

*This book is dedicated to my family
and to the future of freedom in
the United States and around the world.*

CONTENTS

NOT TOO LATE
TO TURN THE TIDE

Why is there so much hatred and violence in our nation?

The Word of God tells us to hate evil, and we should especially avoid evil in our own lives. But we must not hate people who are different from us, who disagree with us, or who are trapped by evil tendencies and unwholesome lifestyles. It's fine to disagree and debate. Ongoing dialogue and important discussions can be healthy. But as Bible-believing Christians, we are called to unwaveringly hold up the truth in love while standing against the hate-filled, deadly outbursts all around us.

I'm convinced the increase in hatred and violence in our nation and around the world is because people have moved far from the redemptive spirit found in Christ. The love of God within us gives us the ability to forgive and understand one another while holding true to our deep convictions with unwavering character.

Christians don't have to be vindictive, destructive, and hateful. The Bible says if you say you love God but hate your brother or sister, you are in darkness (1 John 2:9). No wonder the light is so dim—it's because many Americans and people around the world are filled with darkness.

Even wealth and success are under attack today. Many preachers dare not mention the blessings of God or prosperity for fear they will be critically labeled as "prosperity preachers." We know there are excesses and extremes in every area, but doesn't the Bible talk about God's desire to bless us as His children? Don't all parents want the best and greatest blessings for their children?

God wants us to be so blessed that we become a blessing to the nations of the world. How can we possibly alleviate suffering and help the poor if we don't have the resources to do it? Even those who believe in socialism must have some means of wealth from which to extract the money they wish to disburse.

Legend has it that as the founders signed the Constitution in 1787, Benjamin Franklin observed a painting on the wall in the room in which they had worked so hard to frame that historic document. "I have often . . . in the course of the session . . . looked at that sun behind the President without being able to tell whether it was rising or setting. But now at length I have the happiness to know it is a rising and not a setting sun."[1] It is hard these days not to wonder whether we are still seeing the sunrise or sunset when it comes to freedom as we have been blessed to know it in America.

I have written *The Stream* as a firm warning: Americans must experience a change of heart and mind—and it must come soon, or we are going to see the downfall of freedom and of this once-great nation. If we don't recognize this foolishness and the danger imposed by the hatred of success, blessings, and prosperity, we are going to destroy our ability to meet any legitimate need—along with our future and the future of our children and those we love.

It's not too late for us to turn the tide. We need to release God's love to people all around us, and especially to those with whom we disagree. Only then can expressions of compassion replace hatred and violence. We must boldly demonstrate God's power and especially His love and forgiveness in our nation today.

Many will resonate with the essence of this message but are unsure how they are to respond as salt-and-light kind of people in our present circumstances. In coming chapters we will look at ways we can apply the gospel that has conquered us in a world that needs to be conquered by the love of God. Like Adam and Eve, we have all been given a "garden" to tend with diligent love and oversight. We will share specific ways for believers to stand together against the gates of hellish deception and destruction.

Let us pray fervently for a historic outpouring of the Holy Spirit on His church. It is not too late to renew our culture and restore proven principles. We can be the beginning of the sunrise, not the end. If we will stand up boldly for His truth, live in a way that impacts others, and demonstrate God's character and love, then we can continue to be one nation, under God, indivisible, with liberty and justice for all.

PART
ONE

AMERICA NEEDS HEALING

I am heartsick over what I have observed happening in our great nation in recent years. People appear to be learning very well how to hate others. Outbursts of anger, uncontrollable flare-ups, and temper tantrums are on every newscast and continually fill newspapers and websites. YouTube videos featuring horrific displays of rage are uploaded and viewed by millions.

At the same time, I am convinced that there is reason for hope, because there is One who can turn our mourning to something joyful, not by obscuring the hard truth, but by leading us through the truth of recognition, confession, and repentance. God is ready and able to heal our land if we will humble ourselves, pray and seek His face, and turn from our wicked ways (2 Chronicles 7:14).

Chapter 1

A NATION GONE MAD

As we reflect on the riots in Baltimore and Ferguson, and other outbursts of violence across the nation, we must recognize this is what happens when people forsake God. Whether it's a rogue police officer who guns down an unarmed man in the back (by no means typical of that brave and honorable profession), or a tide of delinquents "protesting" injustice by burning down innocent people's property, the root cause of the chaotic violence is the same as it was in the time of Noah: abandoning God and His unshakable principles. Doing so enslaves one to uncontrolled appetites, sensual practices, and destruction.

Romans 1:18–32 clearly reveals the progression of this rapid descent to depraved thinking and destruction. The first step is the rejection of God. It matters not how often you say, "I believe in God." It matters only what you say daily with your life. Your life must say with every vibrant act, "I adore Him. I worship Him.

I love Him. I believe in Him. I honor Him and I glorify Him, for He is my God." Even while Jesus Christ died on the cross, He said, "My God, My God, why have You forsaken Me?" (Matthew 27:46). Yet with His actions He said, "Even if You forsake me, You are still my Father and my God." That must be the testimony of God's divine creation. He is God. When we do not glorify Him as God, we become vain in our imaginations. Professing ourselves to be wise, we become fools (Romans 1:21–22 KJV).

So how should we respond? Even if they drag all Ten Commandments of Almighty God into the political arena and repudiate them, let us proclaim, "Thus saith the Lord God." If the Supreme Court convenes and decides hell is cruel and unusual punishment, let us stand and teach what the Bible says about hell: there is a hell, and the Bible is the measure by which all societies and all men will be judged.

When you read the Old Testament, you will find that the prophets were considered troublemakers. Most of them were never invited back for a second meeting. They were not popular. Real truth-tellers have seldom been popular, and the Bible has not been popular. They stoned the Old Testament prophets. They killed the apostles. They beheaded John the Baptist. Tradition says they beheaded the apostle Paul. Jesus Christ, the only Son of God and the greatest prophet of all time, was crucified. The Bible may not be popular, but it is true. The Bible reveals life as it should be. That's what we need. When we speak truth to a fallen culture, we will not be well liked, but we must stand up for truth and freedom.

America is great not because of her land or her people. America's greatness is not in our military or materials. It's not in our mechanical or mental greatness. America's greatness is in God.

Our Founding Fathers never conceived a nation separated from God. We are seeing a movement today to separate God from government and from our society. Yet America is built on God. When America gets too intelligent for God, she becomes unintelligent. When she gets too big for God, she shrinks. When she divorces herself from God, she crumbles into the dust. When America forsakes the guidance of God, she is dead.

When we speak truth to a fallen culture, we will not be well liked, but we must stand up for truth and freedom.

We must return to that which our fourth president, James Madison, called on his fellow Americans to trust: "The guardianship and guidance of that Almighty Being whose power regulates the destiny of nations, whose blessings have been so conspicuously dispensed to this rising republic, and to whom we are bound to address our devout gratitude for the past, as well as our fervent supplications and best hopes for the future."[1]

We are clearly witnessing the judgment and wrath of God revealed against all ungodliness as we see people given over to ravenous and demonic appetites and practices. The greatest horror occurs when God's standard is discarded and, as Romans 1:25 says, His truth is exchanged for a lie. So it is that the highest human authorities in this land have been making such awful decisions. There is great reason to mourn for a nation gone mad. And yet, as we will see, there is still hope.

Chapter 2

MOBOCRACY IN THE HEARTLAND

Against the backdrop of a controversial killing of a black man in St. Louis and seething rage across the United States, a young lawyer stood before a small group of men and delivered a speech that would make him famous.

"If destruction be our lot," he proclaimed, "we must ourselves be its author and finisher. As a nation of freemen, we must live through all time, or die by suicide."

The young man was Abraham Lincoln in the year 1838. The black man was Francis McIntosh, a freedman who had been chained to a tree and burned to death by a white mob. The Civil War wouldn't officially begin for over two decades, but the twenty-eight-year-old Lincoln already recognized one of the warning signs of an unraveling society: disregard for the rule of law.

Lincoln continued,

I hope I am over wary; but if I am not, there is, even now, something of ill-omen amongst us. I mean the increasing disregard for law which pervades the country; the growing disposition to substitute the wild and furious passions, in lieu of the sober judgment of Courts; and the worse than savage mobs, for the executive ministers of justice. This disposition is awfully fearful in any community; and that it now exists in ours, though grating to our feelings to admit, it would be a violation of truth, and an insult to our intelligence, to deny. Accounts of outrages committed by mobs, form the every-day news of the times.

Lincoln was not "over wary." His concerns would be played out repeatedly until the entire nation exploded into bloody war. Unfortunately, we are again witnessing "something of an ill-omen amongst us" as mobs periodically assemble in various communities across the country, engaging in acts of violence, theft, and swelling unrest.

We are experiencing the attempted destruction of life and liberty in our own heartland. It is all-out rebellion against the rule of law. For years we have seen blatant disregard of laws, from our borders to our very halls of governance. The root of it all is setting aside God's Word, His Law, and disregarding His counsel. At this moment there are evil men who intend to set our nation on fire, burning up forever the greatest national expression of freedom's beauty ever witnessed by mortal man. America, with all of its ills, failures, and need for correction from time to time, is still the greatest example of a nation established on the rule of law as revealed in sacred Scriptures.

Right now in our country, some foolishly zealous people are encouraging a revolt against the rule of law and accusing those who risk their lives seeking to protect our citizens as though they were targets to be attacked, discredited, and destroyed. Many are simply ignorant of the facts, but others are intentional provocateurs, manipulating the media and the crowd for their own selfish gain. Still others are agents of evil, stirring up passions to provoke violence, as exemplified by death chants against police officers. This is worse than nonsense. It is terrorism at home!

Again, Lincoln recognized this destructive spirit:

When men take it in their heads today, to hang gamblers, or burn murderers, they should recollect, that, in the confusion usually attending such transactions, they will be as likely to hang or burn someone who is neither a gambler nor a murderer as one who is; and that, acting upon the example they set, the mob of tomorrow, may, and probably will, hang or burn some of them by the very same mistake. And not only so; the innocent, those who have ever set their faces against violations of law in every shape, alike with the guilty, fall victims to the ravages of mob law; and thus it goes on, step by step, till all the walls erected for the defense of the persons and property of individuals, are trodden down, and disregarded. But all this even, is not the full extent of the evil. By such examples, by instances of the perpetrators of such acts going un-punished, the lawless in spirit, are encouraged to become lawless in practice; and having been used to no restraint, but dread of punishment, they thus become, absolutely unrestrained. Having ever regarded Government as their deadliest bane, they make a jubilee of the suspension of its operations; and pray for nothing so much, as its total annihilation.

After the tragedy in Ferguson, Missouri, President Obama's actions seemed as if he were seeking to undermine the Supreme Court, Congress, and even our justice system. His remarks condemning police officers who were proven to have acted justly and his quick association with supposed victims who, when the facts came forth, were proven to be in the wrong, play a significant part in the lawless spirit pervading our land today. The president may have been playing to the populace, but he was undermining the very constitution he was entrusted to protect. Politicians towing this line will win friends among the mobs but alienate an even greater number of honest citizens, as Lincoln noted:

> Good men, men who love tranquility, who desire to abide by the laws, and enjoy their benefits, who would gladly spill their blood in the defense of their country; see-ing their property destroyed; their families insulted, and their lives endangered; their persons injured; and seeing nothing in prospect that forebodes a change for the bet-ter; become tired of, and disgusted with, a Government

that offers them no protection; and are not much averse to a change in which they imagine they have nothing to lose. Thus, then, by the operation of this mobocractic spirit, which all must admit, is now abroad in the land, the strongest bulwark of any Government, and particularly of those constituted like ours, may effectually be broken down and destroyed.

Lincoln took on, as we must, the enemy within. By our own disregard of the Word, wisdom, and counsel of God, we have allowed the enemy of life and freedom to set in motion a tsunami of moral and economic collapse destroying personal responsibility and true freedom. Good people—godly people—must stand up and speak the truth. Pure passion can be misguided and dangerous. We need, as Lincoln pointed out, "general intelligence, sound morality, and in particular, a reverence for the constitution and laws."

This practice of playing to the mobs must end. That means voters must repudiate any politician, regardless of party, who demonstrates this tendency. Instead, we must learn to come together in peace, calm, and unwavering strength to face the enemy for Christ's sake and all who long for and love freedom, or we will watch it vanish from this once-great nation and the world.

Our nation was founded on

This practice of playing to the mobs must end. That means voters must repudiate any politician who demonstrates this tendency.

biblical principles. To these, we must hold. These truths are our only hope, for, as Lincoln concluded, "Upon these let the proud fabric of freedom rest, as the rock of its basis; and as truly as has been said of the only greater institution, 'the gates of hell shall not prevail against it.'"[1]

Chapter 3

MOST PEOPLE

If you watch television, listen to talk radio, or read a newspaper, you will repeatedly hear claims about what "most people" think, followed by some assertion. *Most people* don't like what is happening in our country. *Most people* want change. *Most people* are concerned about national direction, the economy, and the future. And, of course, *most people* are angry about the inaction and ineffectiveness of Congress and other leaders.

Well, I have a question to ask. When are *most people* going to stop just talking and complaining and decide to make the necessary difference by taking action, accepting responsibility, and helping to correct those things that deserve our attention? Let me make it clear: correction begins at home, first in each individual life and then through actions affecting everything in our circle of personal influence. Each one of us can make a positive difference when we assume personal responsibility and make the commitment necessary for correction. If *most people* don't think we are headed in the right direction, then it's time for *most people* to make the commitment to do something about it!

Everyone must understand that the political process is moved and directed not just by those who deliver messages and share their concerns but by those who deliver votes! In our constitutional republic, our national direction, laws, and policies are determined by the power and privilege of choosing representatives—those who pass legislation and establish laws. The democratic process grants us the freedom to influence our future by electing our representatives. Thank God for this great privilege—and may God help us to treasure and understand its value. May the Lord help those who care (who I believe are most people) to stand up and make a difference!

Small special-interest groups obviously wield more power and influence in our day than *most people* because *most people* simply complain but do little, if anything, about the problems. Consider the small percentage of the population in groups who really impact national direction, legislation, and policies—the gay activists, environmentalists, labor unions, teachers unions, the NRA, pro-choice activists, pro-life supporters, big business and corporate lobbyists, the anti–God-and-faith-in-the-public-square crowd, as well as partisan activists. These people deliver with determination.

If we want meaningful, purposeful, positive, effective change to the benefit of all, where must the influence come from? Well, from *most people*! Change comes from those who should care the most about all people. I am referring to the community of faith—those who claim to love God and their neighbors. Christians are the ones who can and should deliver the influence to help determine local, state, and national direction as salt and light influencing every aspect of life (Matthew 5:13–16). It comes first by personal example, then through action or activism, zeal and unwavering determination to change what must be changed through wise counsel, reasonable considerations, and deep-principled convictions.

We can and must choose the best-qualified leaders and insist they also deliver. *Most people* in America claim to believe in God, even though some do not seem to know the God of the Bible because they have substituted religious association for true, personal relationship and cannot be counted on to take a stand. This is sad but true. It is also a fact that the largest part of the US population—professing Christians[1]—has often made the least impact on national direction because they are the least active and deliver the least effect.

But let's cut to the chase. Everyone who professes to believe in Christ as Lord and Savior as the way to life can deliver. Let me be very specific about the faith community. Jewish people believe in the God of Abraham, Isaac, and Jacob and in Old Testament truth. Their numbers are small, but they can and do often deliver with great zeal on behalf of things that they consider important. But the real high-impact delivery crowd that can have the greatest

> *Christians are the ones who can and should deliver the influence to help determine local, state, and national direction as salt and light influencing every aspect of life.*

effect is made up of professing Christians. This certainly includes the evangelicals who claim to have a zeal for God and deep concern for others, as well as independent and mainline denominations, Catholics, Pentecostals, charismatics, and all who profess Christ. In sheer numbers alone, professing Christians are "most people." We are capable of quickly changing everything from the bottom up if we will get serious about delivering what *most people* are capable of and accomplishing meaningful results.

The faith community must not just deliver messages and sermons but become bold witnesses to our nation, demonstrating the love and truth that make a difference because faith has made a difference in each one of us. We can witness government begin to fulfill its proper role serving the people effectively while addressing the serious issues that are of concern to every sensitive citizen.

Chapter 4

IT'S EASIER TO LOVE PETS THAN SOME PEOPLE

We sure love our pets, from dogs and cats to parakeets, tropical fish, and hamsters. Now that Betty and I are empty nesters, our little black dachshund, Princess, has filled our hearts and home with indescribable joy. She would be the ultimate church greeter. She loves everyone! If a robber came to our home, after a few barks directed at him, she would then proceed to lick him to death, tail wagging.

Princess is always excited when we come home, even if we just went out into the garage to check on something. You would think we had been gone for days. She is always glad to be with us and is sad when she is not. Sounds a lot like first love, doesn't it? Pets can show us how we should always love to abide in God's presence. Pets certainly don't do everything right, but most of them love us unconditionally. It seems, oftentimes, even the smallest dog would fight a bear or a lion, trying to protect us.

I love when Princess lies on my chest with her big, brown eyes staring a hole in me. I am certain she is just admiring me. Don't we love it? If you have a dog or a cat, you know that feeling you get when they sit at your feet just gazing at you. No meow or bark is necessary; we know they want something, usually a treat, or perhaps attention or to play, or, on occasion, they have a real need like fresh water or food.

Somehow I think our intent look into the very face of God with deep, inner longing would speak much louder to Him than so much pleading and begging. Our fixation on Him would confirm our absolute faith and confidence in His ability to do all things well and to meet every legitimate need. We all need to readjust our focus. May God help us all to fix our eyes on the standard so we can plow through life without wavering from side to side because of meaningless and damaging distractions and attractions.

So why can pets be much easier to love than people? Pets annoy us when they needlessly bark or relieve themselves at the wrong times in the wrong places. There are ways, however, to stop them from doing this or to easily clean up the mess. But with people it is totally different. Many make so much annoying noise—always complaining, criticizing, begging, bellyaching, refusing personal responsibility, blaming others, and being ungrateful. Come to think of it, Betty and I have never heard Princess yelp a thank you, but we can tell she appreciates our help. This is more than you can say for many people. It's sad but true. It is a fact that many people who have succeeded seem to be controlled by greed. On the other side, however, you seldom hear people express gratitude for the hard-working Americans who pay the majority of taxes that enable government assistance to be offered and legitimate needs met. Instead, people are encouraged to be hostile toward the producers of opportunity, needed products, and prosperity.

People are too often rude, impatient, lovers of themselves, lovers of stuff more than people, full of envy, jealous, disobedient to parents, disrespectful, unloving, unholy, without self-control, haters of good, conceited, lovers of pleasure more than lovers of God, holding to a form of godliness while denying His power (2 Timothy 3:2–5).

What are we to do? Here is God's answer: Trust Him for a miracle of love and grace and remember that but for His grace, there go we. Such were some of us before Christ (1 Corinthians 6:9–11). Even now it is easy for us to slip back into the ways of the world, especially when we take a serious look at those we are commanded to love. It is difficult to stay true to God and His Word when the siren call of this world's atmosphere influences and invites us continually to walk in the ways of rebellion and self-centeredness. The culture's temptations are endless and too often filled with seemingly attractive clatter.

Our only hope is God's help, which He freely offers if we will accept it. By God's grace I have accepted His help, and I will continue to do so. It is not only difficult, but it is absolutely impossible to properly love others as we should unless we seek and allow God's help.

Let's pray together that God will grant us the grace to love people more than pets—as tough as that may be. Remember, "with

God all things are possible" (Matthew 19:26) and "love never fails" (1 Corinthians 13:8). Amazingly, God continues to give me a love for those in dire circumstances and also for those whose ways I do not care for and find difficult to understand. This is not due to any greatness on my part, but it is all a gift from the One who is greater working in me. This inner transformation is what we all need.

PART
TWO

SPIRITUAL AWAKENING IS OUR ONLY HOPE

We will see a new day in America, but only if there is a spiritual awakening. It's quite a different thing to vote for "hope and change" than to experience it. Hope will only come when people's hearts are changed.

As we clearly observe deterioration of freedom as well as of traditional understandings of marriage, family, biblical morality, and sound economic principles, we sense a necessary call to action—and respond we must! While responding, it is critically important to know the essential principles of divine design. These problems have been created by ignoring truth that goes beyond a single culture's ideas on organizing society.

We can't just "fix" things without God-given wisdom. Judging that the problem relates to ignorance of—or depreciation of—

divine principles, we seek to reinstate them in the structures that shape society. We may work to define and clarify them relative to our current situation and then look for leaders in influential spheres who will espouse them—all the while believing that when societal structures align with principles of divine order, life will be better for all.

Chapter 5

BOTTOM-UP, INSIDE-OUT: INTERNAL CHANGE FIRST

Setting up government programs that help people seems like a loving thing to do. After all, we want people (including ourselves) to have the greatest opportunity possible to have a happy and meaningful life. And since helping others makes us feel better, this seems like a win/win strategy. So is there a problem? I think so—at least from the perspective of the Christian who has been commissioned to make the gospel central to everything he or she says or does.

Government assistance can be executed without the gospel, but it will not be fully successful. The principles that make life work better can be discovered and applied by anyone wise enough to observe and learn. But the problem lies with the one trying to apply them. Inevitably these principles will be misused, abused, and maligned by the self-obsessed heart of the individual trying to survive in what it perceives as a threatening environment.

It is not possible outside the gospel to balance the competing interests of human flourishing. Free market principles help create increasing economic growth that makes all of society wealthier and better off, but often those who are greatly benefited appear to overlook the plight of the poor. At the same time, compassion can lead to an inappropriate approach to ending poverty and promoting more equal distribution, but at the cost of limiting opportunities for all. There is a problem in human access of the principles themselves. They require an "invisible hand" of divine love governing them, just as the free market requires what Adam Smith called the "invisible hand" of self-interest.[1]

In one of Jesus's parables, God called a man a fool because in observing the principle of sowing and reaping he was consumed with gathering more and more for his own interests alone (Luke 12:16–21). The same kind of misuse will be true of all the principles found in creation. God's principles are valid. The human heart is defective.

The culprit is not the socialist's philosophy, which seeks to displace democratic capitalism and debunk American exceptionalism. It is the inability of untransformed people to live by the principles of divine order. Apart from the radical application of the gospel of Christ, the human heart will not and cannot live by even the simplest principle without perverting it for its own benefit. This means that reinstating moral and biblical principles into societal structures is at best a temporary solution. In a society where the vast majority of people are unfamiliar with the transforming power of the gospel or at least the ethical effects rippling from it, the reforms will be like the Eighteenth Amendment and Prohibition. They will be repealed either by legislation or by covert revolution.

As Christians concerned about our civic responsibilities, we have discovered a principle higher than all others and one that is necessary to implement the principles of divine order without abuse. We can neither neglect this nor assume others can successfully operate in divine principles without it. In the gospel of Jesus Christ we encounter a kind of love that is otherworldly and transforming. God loved us when we were undeserving and uncaring. He did for us what we couldn't do for ourselves, and He included us in His plan to bless the world through the loving sacrifice of Jesus, His Son. We are the proclaimers of this great love story. When others hear it in their hearts, they, too, are changed and empowered to live without enslaving fear.

Once we are captured by this godly love, we are empowered to operate in it. We can love people without depending upon those we love to give back. The problem with trying to change society with human love is that it will inevitably lead to disillusionment. Those who should appreciate the sacrifice made to help them have a better life will instead reject the divine principles, concluding they require too much responsibility. Often they will resent the reformer for interfering with their lives. When love is not returned, it dies. In its place will grow seeds of bitterness and skepticism. The reformer becomes a cynic.

Most Christians will readily admit that internal transformation precedes external change, but they emphasize the external because it is more obvious and measurable. (In our culture, if it can't be measured, it doesn't count.) The visible, external crises of lost religious freedom, mounting debt, governmental encroachment, and unjust taxation cry for attention, and these issues are serious. But they are simply the results of eroding civil government due to the lack of the internal influence of a gospel mandate to subdue the earth by making disciples of all peoples. When we assume the gospel we are presuming on reality. If we are going to assume, let's assume that when hearts are changed by God's love, the society will change—first at home, then in the community, the state, the nation, and the world. Those who treat the gospel as optional don't understand its totality. It is an incomplete gospel that deals only with the eternal destiny of the soul and leaves unaffected the world in which we sojourn.

I don't know if the early church strategized to transform the empire of Rome. We have scant evidence of such. They were more obviously enamored with being a part of a new nation that came from heaven, filled them with the love of God, and empowered them with the same Spirit who raised Jesus from death. The early church infiltrated Rome and affected the known world like leaven invades a whole lump of dough. It was and is the kingdom of God. This kingdom is still the only nation with a heavenly mandate. It is the only nation that can affect all other nations. The Lord Jesus sits on the throne. His message gives meaning to existence. His victory will be culminated on earth. Why would we labor outside of this mission? If the kingdom of God is the key to the solution, why would we settle for less?

Many who profess faith fail to trust in the power of the gospel. We have every reason to doubt any gospel that doesn't move a person from his or her fascination with self, from thinking that spirituality is only about going to heaven, from bondage to emotional and behavioral addictions, and from individualistic preoccupation. But the true gospel that captured the early Christians empowered them to so exalt Jesus in their daily lives that a by-product was the transformation of whatever culture they were in. These believers were truly salt and light wherever they went. These passionate disciples who were abiding in the Word of God dramatically affected societal rot and darkness. These believers somehow knew that the love they had received from God was more powerful than political kingdoms, tyrants, and death.

It still is. God's love is the only power that can and will defeat all forms of evil. Why would we ignore it when we want to see evil defeated in our generation?

Could we be victims of our need to be significant? We are problem solvers. We can find a measure of significance if we come up with a solution to the immediate problems that face us. The problem with world-changers is the temptation to compete with the One who has already come to change the world. He did it not by becoming a hero to His culture but by cutting the root of human bondage. His followers, who changed their world (like Paul), did it by telling a simple story that seemed silly to

> *God's love is the only power that can and will defeat all forms of evil.*

the thinkers and foolish to the religious. Their primary concerns were not the economic and political conditions of their day. They proclaimed a new Lord and a new kingdom that would confront and offer the blessings of change to all nations. They were not obsessed with being world-changers. They were obsessed by proclaiming the name and message of their Lord. They were committed to enhancing His reputation. As a result of their passion, cultures changed. Like leaven in a lump of dough, the power of the gospel works unnoticed until the whole lump is penetrated.

When we see deplorable conditions in our society, we cannot be content to offer a temporary fix. Internal transformation *must* precede external change. Only the New Testament gospel does that. "It is the power of God unto salvation [deliverance]" (Romans 1:16 KJV). Believers are commanded by Christ to be bold witnesses, releasing the power of transforming truth.

Chapter 6

HOPE AND CHANGE

The only hope for America lies in the effective witness and influence of the local church for the transformation of the individual, not in the power of government or social movements. A political slogan of "hope and change" is a false substitute for spiritual hope and godly change.

The church in America precedes the foundation of our nation. The Pilgrims left the religious persecution they endured in their European homes to come to America and establish a new life where they were free to worship. One of the first structures in precolonial settlements was the church building, which stood as a place not only to worship but also to meet with neighbors, engage in community activities, elect officials, and dispense charity. Many of our country's great historical events and movements, from national independence to civil rights, started or flourished in churches.

Today the local church still stands as a primary source of strength in communities, second only to the family. Whether it is in a centuries-old cathedral in New England or in a converted shopping strip in southern California, people still need a church.

Consider the wide range of services the church provides: fellowship with friends, consolation after the loss of a loved one, direction in difficult times, food for the hungry, clothes for the needy, shelter for the homeless, and so much more. Most churches provide a secure and stable sense of family, an atmosphere of belonging, and evidence that God cares.

Governments may attempt to aid disadvantaged families and neighborhoods through financial assistance, but positive and permanent change seldom occurs simply by handing out cash. Without the personal touch of people who genuinely care, social welfare usually becomes a wasteful tax burden. But when finances are used to fuel the work of an existing core of concerned people, such as the church, the impact is visible and meaningful. Government has a role in our lives, but its role is limited. When the church accepts its divinely ordained role, there is no limit to the positive influence it can have on individuals and the nation.

By empowering the local church to further its mission of helping our fellow man, we are empowering a nation to be strong. Through the power of positive human touch, lives are redeemed, families restored, and communities revitalized.

So why are Judeo-Christian principles under so much assault? The forces of religious intolerance appear to be gaining ground, but this may not be the fight in which Christians wish to engage. Christians around the world have suffered brutally for centuries, from the Roman Empire to the Soviet Empire. Even today believers across the Middle East and beyond are being tortured, maimed, and killed for their faith. America still stands as a nation where people can worship freely. Yet this liberty could be forfeited because of indifference or lack of commitment on the part of believers.

Tearing down all of our national monuments that contain religious references or imagery would be tragic. But even if the separation-of-church-and-state enforcers destroyed the statues of Moses in and on the Supreme Court in Washington, DC, in the Library of Congress, and in the Ronald Reagan Building, they could not remove the legacy of the God of Moses from people's hearts. Even if the floor of the National Archives Building were covered to conceal the Ten Commandments, the ears of our children would not be covered from hearing the biblical principles contained in those simple instructions.

The windows of the US Capitol could be shattered to eliminate the image of George Washington kneeling in prayer, but the power of prayer will continue to shatter the destructive forces in the lives of hurting people. Reciting "one nation under God" in the pledge is not nearly as important as knowing that this nation must be under God's direction and protection. References to Almighty God could be cut out of all the speeches, writings, and monuments of every great American leader, but the influence of Almighty God can never be eliminated. Our major concern should always be living the Ten Commandments, not just defending where they are engraved. "In God We Trust" inscribed on our coins is not as much of an issue as whether we trust God with all of our hearts. These are the real issues at hand.

Americans know that our freedom is bought with a price. Many lives have been sacrificed to stave off the evil forces that seek to suppress our freedom of religion, expression, movement, and thought. In my lifetime alone, Nazis, communists, anarchists, and radical Muslims have sought to steal some of the most basic freedoms that Americans take for granted.

Voting is not just an inherent right or a mere privilege, but it is our responsibility. Edward Everett Hale, former chaplain of the US Senate, said, "I am only one—but I am one. I cannot do everything, but I still can do something."[1] The most basic "something" we can do is to vote.

Voting is not just an inherent right or a mere privilege, it is our responsibility.

All citizens should get out and cast their votes on the issues that live beyond today and will affect our children and grandchildren. Someone will determine our future; why not Christians? We have the power not only to change people's lives today but also to help shape the future for generations to come. The church can be the most powerful agent of positive change, both inside the sanctuary and outside. Through the gospel of Jesus Christ, we can impact individuals. Through a bold commitment to godly principles, compassionate action to help those in need, and informed participation in the electoral process, we can impact our nation.

Chapter 7

THE IMPORTANCE OF GRATITUDE

E very year Americans celebrate Thanksgiving. In 1621, the pilgrims of the Plymouth Plantation in Massachusetts gathered with Native Americans in a feast of gratitude, even though they had been through many years of drought, disease, and death. They knew they had many hard years ahead of them, yet they paused to give thanks to God for the bountiful harvest that year.

Thanksgiving celebrations continued over the next two hundred years, and some presidents issued Thanksgiving proclamations. President Abraham Lincoln made Thanksgiving an official national holiday in 1863, when our country was in the throes of the Civil War. There may have been no darker time in our nation's history, yet Lincoln called on Americans to thank God for the blessings He had bestowed upon them.

A few years later, in 1880, President Rutherford B. Hayes issued his Thanksgiving Proclamation, which said, in part:

> Health, wealth, and prosperity throughout all our borders; peace, honor, and friendship with all the world; firm and faithful adherence by the great body of our population to the principles of liberty and justice which have made our greatness as a nation, and to the wise institutions and strong frame of government and society which will perpetuate it—for all these let the thanks of a happy and united people, as with one voice, ascend in devout homage to the Giver of All Good.[1]

Today most of us would find the living conditions of 1880 deplorable. Electricity was in its infancy. Just one year earlier, Thomas Edison had invented the incandescent light bulb. Heating and cooling were things of the future. People rode on horses or in buggies. Health care was crude and life expectancy a mere forty years. The losses of the Civil War were still fresh. Yet even in conditions that would render us miserable, people found cause to give thanks to God.

Unfortunately, it's easy for us to harden our hearts to God's blessings, even in our advanced society. People with smartphones take to the streets to protest working conditions that would be considered luxurious in most countries. Gratitude has little to do with our circumstances and everything to do with our hearts.

The apostle Paul understood this truth when he wrote, "I have learned to be content whatever the circumstances. I know what it is to be in need, and I know what it is to have plenty. I have learned the secret of being content in any and every situation, whether well fed or hungry, whether living in plenty or in want. I can do all this through him who gives me strength" (Philippians 4:11–13 NIV). Paul and Silas actually sang praises to God after being beaten and imprisoned in Philippi for preaching the gospel (Acts 16:25). As a result of their gratitude, they were freed and the jailer and his entire family were saved. The city experienced the power of God's love.

What is true contentment? It's not sloth, tolerance of oppression, or satisfaction with poverty, abuse, or other damaging things. It's seeing every event in our lives—whether it brings pleasure or pain—as a part of God's work in the light of eternity. When Paul wrote, "God causes all things to work together for good to those who love God, to those who are called according to His purpose" (Romans 8:28), he obviously had in mind the hardships, pain, and suffering we experience. Good things don't need to be worked together for good—they already are good. We must learn to be thankful, even in our need. Learning to think this way is not easy. Without faith, this perspective on our circumstances may seem crazy. But when our ultimate end is to glorify God, then we can receive even suffering as a great blessing.

Gratitude has little to do with our circumstances and everything to do with our hearts.

These days many Americans are much more likely to have a spirit of ingratitude. If we only see lack instead of blessing, then we will be perpetually discontent. In our society, that discontent often breeds malcontent. No matter how many comforts one has, there is always someone with more. There is always someone who has a bigger house or a newer car or a better job or better health. The one who lacks the spirit of gratitude may resent the prosperity of others more than he enjoys his own.

Discontent comes from failing to cultivate a spirit of gratitude. Even though our nation has high unemployment, most of us have our basic needs met, with some left over. We enjoy freedoms that earlier generations could only imagine. We have eradicated diseases that killed millions of people in the last century. We live longer than any generation before us. Average people enjoy more food, technology, leisure, and health care than most of the wealthiest kings and queens in history.

Compare our lot to that of the early Americans. They lost love ones to disease, malnutrition, and exposure, yet they were thankful to have survived. Of course, we should be glad that we don't worry about mere survival. But if we don't cultivate a spirit of gratitude, then we will forget to be thankful for even the most delightful blessings. We must learn to "consider it all joy," as James said (James 1:2).

If we want to truly be happy, we must value everyone.

The inability to find joy even in hardship creates a sense of entitlement and breeds jealousy, anger, and even hatred. This leads to a devaluation of life as we learn to resent others who have more than we do. Instead of viewing those who are successful as possible role models, we see them as enemies to be destroyed. We have seen this discontent spill into the streets in recent years. Sometimes there are legitimate issues, but more often it has become a demonstration of rampant rage.

We are no longer a "happy and united people," as President Hayes said. Good law-enforcement officials have been wanton targets of this discontent. This is not healthy for individuals or society. If we want to truly be happy, we must value everyone. This begins by finding contentment and gratitude in our own lives.

Chapter 8

RETURN TO WISDOM

Christians must recognize that a house divided against itself cannot stand (Mark 3:25). Church leadership must stop fighting over internal differences and become supernaturally united by love, concern for others, and fulfilling God's kingdom purpose, while rejecting the godless worldview being pushed on the culture.

It's obvious that American leadership lacks the wisdom that comes only from above. These are realities we face:

- Americans are divided in numerous ways.
- When God is diminished, government grows.
- We can either believe politicians' promises or rely on faith in divine providence.
- We must choose between proven biblical principles or the ever-drifting opinions of secularists.

- There is an all-out assault on faith, absolutes, and any mention of God in public.
- Moral standards have been rejected, marriage has been redefined, and anything goes in sexual practices.
- Protection of the innocent and innocence has lost all value.
- Excess in government spending is bankrupting the country, robbing future generations of the opportunity to succeed through honest labor.
- Freedom and responsibility are being exchanged for dependence and entitlement.

An excessive, ineffective, all-powerful state is replacing a free, personally responsible citizenry. National direction is being determined by special-interest groups who demand "rights" while denying the legitimate rights of others. As a result, opportunity, productivity, and even the promise of meaningful employment are being destroyed.

Recognizing the serious problems we face, Christians must stop arguing among ourselves and stand together as an unshakable, spiritually united body of true believers. We must reject the thought that the spiritual is to be separated from the governmental. Transformed people transform the culture while standing up for what is right. Let it be said of believers today that we feared no man and no power, and we gave no ground to the enemy.

Take a moment to consider the effect of Christian principles in the development of the United States of America. Christian influence on government was primarily responsible for the Declaration of Independence, the Constitution, and the Bill of

Rights. These are three of the most significant documents in the history of governments on the earth, and all three show the marks of significant Christian influence in the foundational ideas of how governments should function. These foundations of our country did not come about as a result of the "do church, not politics" view.

Charles Thomson was the permanent Secretary of the Continental Congress for more than fifteen years. He and John Hancock were the only two to sign the original Declaration of Independence, known as the Dunlap Broadsides, which were originally printed on the night of July 4, 1776. Most of the signatories didn't sign until August. After retiring from public office in 1789, Thomson spent twenty years translating the Septuagint Bible from Greek into English.

A historian later wrote about the character of this highly influential and spiritual man, "It is scarcely necessary to make any further reference to Thomson's religious belief. He had accepted the truths of Christianity in his early youth, and his whole life displayed a beautiful, upright character that was a constant inspiration to his friends. He not only became a Christian in the usual sense of the term; but he retired from public life, and for twenty-five years, was a solitary student of divine truth."[1]

Thomson is just one of many godly men who were instrumental in the foundation of our nation. If our founders had adopted the "do church, not politics" view, we might not have a country today. But we do, because Christians realized that if they could influence laws and governments for good they would be obeying the command of their Lord, "Let your light shine before men in such a way that they may see your good works, and glorify your Father who is in heaven" (Matthew 5:16).

The choice is clear: we can live in freedom under God or in bondage under any other source, which amounts to a modern-day Pharaoh. Paul told the New Testament church that the things that happened to Israel are an example for us (1 Corinthians 10:6). Surely you remember how God delivered the people from bondage in order to lead them into the land of blessing, freedom, and fruitfulness. Our God is a God who blesses those living in His shadow. Only unbelief and disobedience to His Word can hinder the blessings He freely offers through His Son. "If the Son makes you free, you will be free indeed" (John 8:36).

True believers understand that hearts and minds must be transformed by the power of God and by witnessing the visible manifestation of His life through the fruit of the Holy Spirit. Now is the time to rise and shine with the glory of the Lord upon us (Isaiah 60:1). Concerned Christians must support leaders who understand the reality of spiritual warfare and the importance of a Christian worldview. This does not mean we impose our faith on others, merely that we choose representatives who reflect our values. That is both the benefit and danger of democracy.

Sadly, I believe that inept, self-serving, corrupt leaders actually do reflect the values of many people. That's why the church must rise up, courageously and compassionately demonstrating and defending the love of Christ. This we know for sure: Christ left us here as His witnesses on this earth for His glory and kingdom purpose. The moment Christians decide to stand together as the family of God, the forces of hell will tremble and truth will win!

PART

THREE

FREEDOM IS GOD'S GIFT TO MANKIND

As God's children, we should be wise overseers of His creation, faithfully proclaiming the life and liberty that only He offers. True freedom is living under God's control, not under the control of any other power.

"It was for freedom that Christ set us free," the apostle Paul tells us (Galatians 5:1). We are created to be free. But there is a second part to Paul's statement: ". . . therefore keep standing firm and do not be subject again to a yoke of slavery." With freedom comes responsibility for our choices and actions. If we hope to preserve freedom, we must embrace these responsibilities.

God values our freedom so much that He gives us the power to reject Him. The Old Testament chronicles the consequences of this freedom. God's chosen people cycled in and out of slavery as they vacillated between obedience and apathy or defiance. When we reject Him today, we fall under the bondage of sin. But God does not abandon us to our bondage. By bearing the brunt of sin, He gives us the option to be reconciled with Him. Ultimate freedom is freedom in Christ. At the same time, God has revealed ways for societies to restrain evil and achieve some measure of corporate freedom, even when some people reject Him individually.

In free societies the government both protects and submits to the rule of law. It conforms to those realities outside it, including to the roles of individuals, families, the church, and other institutions. Free societies protect private property. They allow their citizens to participate in the political process, to make basic economic choices, to speak their minds (even when wrong), and to freely exercise religious faith. In the long run, our political, economic, and religious freedoms stand or fall together.

Chapter 9

KISSING FREEDOM GOOD-BYE

We can kiss freedom in America good-bye unless those who say they know and love God stand together against the forces of evil. If we don't act now, it will be too late to halt evil's intent. Satan's goal has always been the destruction of life and freedom, and in our day he often appears to be winning.

Can you believe the decisions that are currently being made by our nation's elected leaders? They act as if they are promoting rebellion against wise and godly thinking. Evil is now called good, and good is called evil, just as Isaiah said (5:20).

Concerned Americans can surely stand together in defense of freedom. The future of freedom will be determined with godly diversity coming together in supernatural unity to stand up for transforming truth. We must refuse to give the enemy another inch of the ground God has told us to oversee.

In our present day, enemies of faith and true freedom don't

even want to acknowledge the supernatural power that influenced America's birth or the importance of God, faith, family, and the principles necessary for freedom. Their coalition of hostile forces, however different, diverse, or distinct, refuses to be divided. They stand together hell-bent in opposition to undeniable, absolute, transforming truth. Sadly, those who know the truth and hold to the importance of it seem unable to work together as a family standing in behalf of faith and true freedom. The exaltation of truth and freedom has transformed people and blessed nations throughout the ages.

It's now time for people who understand the value of faith and freedom and its foundation to stand together like a mighty army, an undeniable spiritual force. The very term *freedom* implies the potential for abuse. For freedom's sake, for your sake, and for your posterity, do not assault, attack, and destroy freedom in a foolish attempt to curb or control abuse. Don't destroy freedom's fertile fields of opportunity because of neglect or abuse on the part of any individual. We must reclaim the land of promise birthed through faith, prayer, and personal sacrifice to bless the American people and the nations of the world. Our freedom can only be preserved with the same determination, diligence, and supernatural unity Jesus prayed for (John 17) and champions of freedom so well understand.

Ronald Reagan made many great statements concerning freedom, including this one: "Freedom is never more than one generation away from extinction. We don't pass it on to our children in the bloodstream. It must be fought for, protected, and handed on to them to do the same, or one day we will spend our sunset years telling our children and our children's children what it was once like in the United States when men were free."[1]

I do not want to be found among those who will be asked what we were doing when freedom died. By the grace of God, with His help and the help of those who share common concerns and with Christians of conviction, I will not be indifferent and allow freedom to die on my watch. I will continue to pray, preach, and openly call for a return to God-given principles.

The short term matters. Politicians who violate these principles should be replaced with politicians who defend and apply them properly. If we want lasting change, however, we have to restore the rest of the culture too.

Politics can shape the culture, but ultimately politics reflect the culture. People of faith can still vote, but we have been culturally marginalized. Things that were once considered part of society have been co-opted by the government. This has had a devastatingly negative impact. Marriage is a church institution, but it has been taken over and nearly destroyed by the government. Abortion is a moral issue, but it has been politicized. Even welfare and health care were once strongholds of religious responsibility, but now religious organizations are being forced to forsake their convictions or get out of the business of helping others.

This politicization will lead to the collapse of these issues and institutions unless they are seriously reformed. We need to prepare because either way—courageous reform or disastrous collapse—there will be a growing need for nongovernmental charitable programs that can truly help the elderly, the poor, the handicapped, and the otherwise disadvantaged. Christians will need to play a larger role in helping the needy in our communities, and this will give us an opportunity to properly rebuild culture and civil society.

Profound cultural change will only come from an outward expression of an inward change. We need a spiritual revival of our hearts and minds, which starts in our churches, changes our communities, and reforms the culture. We need changed people and championed prayer before we can expect godly principles and policies. Whenever the church is in tune with the Holy Spirit, the kingdom of God breaks through in the culture. We must face these issues now if we and our children are to live free.

Chapter 10

PREACHERS, PRIESTS, AND POLITICS

I think America is headed in the wrong direction—straight into the ditch of out-of-control debt, with government agencies enforcing rules that were never passed and have even been rejected by Congress. Much of the media and population continually mock the God of the Bible, diminishing the value of marriage, family, and even innocent life. Blind leaders have our blind nation headed over a cliff. Thank God some representatives and preachers and priests see what is coming, as do many people, and they want to help right our ship of state.

I am hopeful, and I have good news to announce from God. He is the shelter from the storm and the Shepherd who will lead us to lie down in green pastures, beside still waters, and restore us body and soul, while preparing a table before us with goodness and mercy following us even in the presence of many enemies and accusers.

Whenever issues of national and moral importance (which have now been made political) are addressed by a religious leader, we hear the outcry, "Stay out of politics!" In other words, they say ministers must avoid real-life issues, problems, and challenges on the national stage by never standing up with hopeful, helpful solutions. The truth is, Christians, all people of faith, and certainly preachers of the Word of God are obligated to speak out boldly and to stand for their convictions. People with a secular, humanist, God-denying view that assaults Judeo-Christian biblical views and diminishes the importance of founding documents are continually organizing in every community. They force their views on the population through protests and radical political activism while never giving up an inch of their sacred turf, however *unsacred* it actually is. They expect the church community to shut up and go back to sleep and keep our faith to ourselves.

Christians, all people of faith, and certainly preachers of the Word of God are obligated to speak out boldly and to stand for their convictions.

There are even a few people who love God who have asked me, "James, are you getting too political?" Exactly what does that mean? Am I concerned? Yes. Do I care? Yes. Do I love God and people? Yes. Do I want to assist the suffering, homeless, and elderly? Yes. That is why I am compelled to speak. I am commissioned by God and His Word to speak, to put a trumpet to my lips (Hosea 8:1), to sound an alarm on the holy mountain (Joel 2:1), to warn the people, stand in the gap, repair the breach, rebuild the walls, restore the foundation, and faithfully present the one reliable standard—the Word of the living God. I am called to preach "the way, and the truth, and the life" (John 14:6). I can and I will do no other. Now is the time to call a solemn assembly, to rend our hearts and not our garments (Joel 2:13). No more religious pretense. It is time to stop just honoring God with our lips (Matthew 15:8) and begin honoring Him with all of our hearts, with everything that is in us. As Christians, it is of utmost importance that we not just try to tell people how to live, but actually show them how to live by our example. New Testament believers were so full of life and love they turned their upside-down world right side up. I am challenging all ministers, priests, people of God, and leaders to consider doing the same also.

At the Freedom Rally in Dallas, Texas, in 1979, I delivered a declaration concerning my stand for freedom. These words still stand true today, and are needed more than ever before:

Why am I here? I am here to announce my intention to maintain freedom. To blast the avowed enemies of freedom. To challenge the assassins of freedom. To demand the rights in our freedom. To enlist an army of defenders of freedom. To enlighten the minds of people concerning the tragic losses of freedom; to file my objectives concerning the abuses of freedom. To generate concern for reapers for freedom. To gain a new hold on freedom. I'm here to halt the infringements against freedom. To implement ways to maintain our freedom. To insist on the full privilege of freedom. To justify the defense of freedom. To keep freedom alive. To lead the champions of freedom. To magnify the importance of freedom; muzzle the voices against freedom; nurse the most recent wounds of freedom; oppose the foes of freedom; object to the losses of freedom; protect our freedom; question the decisions against freedom. I'm here to resist those who oppose freedom; stop the assault on freedom; tear off the shackles on freedom; unite freedom's warriors; voice the cry for freedom; vote for freedom; wrestle the foes of freedom; expose the attack on freedom; yell for the cause of freedom; zero in on the destroyers of freedom.

That rally helped restore our television program to the ABC affiliate in Dallas and undo the so-called Fairness Doctrine that was so destructive to freedom. I continued:

I believe America is great. America is not great because of her land or her people. America's greatness is not in the military or materials of our country. It's not in mechanical or mental greatness, but America's greatness is in God. Our Founding Fathers never conceived a nation separated from God. We have a move on today to separate God from government, and God from our society. That is not why America was founded. America is built on God. When America gets too intelligent for God, she has become unintelligent. When she gets too big for God, she is too big. When she divorces herself from God, she will crumble into the dust. When America forsakes the guidance of God, she is dead.

As a minister of the gospel and one called to deliver the truth that sets us free and keeps us free, I will *endorse* biblical truth, love, compassion, courage, convictions, strong marriages and families, and the importance of everyone assuming responsibility for their actions as well as influencing local and national direction. I support the Constitution as our founders established it. I do not endorse candidates or parties, but ministers certainly have a God-given right to do so and no one understood this better than our Founding Fathers. When a preacher or highly visible person endorses a candidate, that is their right and we should all respect them even if we disagree with their opinion. We can disagree without being hateful. I will talk to, counsel, challenge, pray for and with any candidate running for any office or holding any office. I will love them all even if I firmly disagree. But I will not be a soggy, mushy, mealymouthed, inspire-no-one preacher. Never!

I will *exhort* by speaking up and speaking out, because that's what preachers are called by God to do. Woe is me and all of us as ministers if we do not. When we do not proclaim truth and liberty throughout the land, we have failed both God and man. "Shout it from the housetops" (Matthew 10:27 NLT) or the "rocks will cry out against us" (Luke 19:40). The fact is the Word of God is carved in the stone on buildings throughout Washington, DC, and it continues to testify while some pulpits have gone silent and the pews become a sanctimonious mortuary. Ministers must not be timid and fearful or they will have a church filled with spineless, fear-filled people who will never become a "city set on a hill" (Matthew 5:14).

I will *embrace* sound principles upon which we can build our lives, families, and future. I support what has been proven to work throughout human history to the real benefit of people, not some idea or suggestion that reduces humanity and human beings to something less than God created us to be. Lives as well as buildings must be established on a solid foundation and today as with the city of New Orleans, many Americans and, yes, politicians are hell-bent on building their future not only on sand, but on sand below sea level.

I will *expose* evil, damaging practices, and bad policy, since most media and many academics do not seem to believe in evil and obviously some lawmakers and even ministry leaders don't seem to either. In other words, the three little pigs and Red Riding Hood need to learn there is no big, bad wolf, and while at it chunk the Bible along with the children's stories out the window and continue living in a failing, fantasyland dream world—nightmare! So for these who don't believe the Bible and obvious truth, let me address what I mean by bad policy. If it doesn't work or isn't sustainable, no matter how sincere the instigators, stop the madness! It is worse than suicidal; it becomes murder—death to people and a secure future.

I will *encourage* every person to assume responsibility for their own lives and decisions, and to diligently seek to assist others. I encourage qualified people to serve, whether on a homeowners' association, PTA, school board, or local, state, or national office. We need the best to run and be elected to serve for the benefit of the people. It is our duty—actually a calling. I encourage every citizen to be very well informed (commitment is required—you must consider what is best for everyone), and be actively involved. Vote faithfully and with conviction for those who hold truth, freedom, and sound principles dear. Do not vote just for one issue or out of mere personal preference, damaging party loyalty, or attractive personalities. Consider the whole package—vote principle, not just preference. There has only been one perfect candidate—Jesus—and He won't run. He rules in the lives of those submitted to Him! I encourage everyone to recognize how valuable and important they are, because I see them all through the eyes of the God some refuse to acknowledge or love. Because of this twisted view, people are loved less.

I will *endure*—I am in the race to win, not just an election, not the approval of men, but the "race God has set before us all" (Hebrews 12:1). This is a race for the full expression of the life, love, and liberty only God can give that people are to share. I will stand and keep standing.

To the people and all political candidates, I say: "If you are going to get beat up or beat, let it happen because you are standing boldly in behalf of what is best for God and country—for people." So if you are asking me to explain in succinct words what I am trying to do, here is my answer: I want to inspire everyone to first get on our face before God and then stand on our feet for God.

This is the stand I took then and continue to take today. All believers must stand up and not allow the enemies of freedom to push us aside. We can be the difference our nation, and even our world, needs in order to thrive.

Chapter 11

FREEDOM MUST BE PROTECTED

The framers of the Constitution knew that the freedom they offered demanded responsible citizens. At the close of the Constitutional Convention of 1787, Benjamin Franklin was asked an important question as he left Independence Hall on the final day of the meeting in Philadelphia. A woman asked Franklin, "Well, doctor, what have we got? A republic or a monarchy?" He wisely answered, "A republic, if you can keep it."[1]

Benjamin Franklin, as well as the other Founding Fathers of our nation, understood that true liberty requires support from principled statesmen who are actively engaged in the task of governing themselves, encouraging all citizens to hold fast to truths espoused in the Declaration of Independence. If we want to be free, we must learn to govern ourselves. Ill-informed, irresponsible people cannot hold on to freedom's blessings. Living under

God's control allows us not only to enjoy the privileges of freedom but also to protect them.

With deep conviction, I believe we are on the verge of losing freedom's blessings because we have too few informed and responsible citizens. More than that, the church has not understood the importance of living under the control of God with the powerful Spirit of God providing the strength for us to enjoy and protect our freedom.

Jesus said the gates of hell—deception, defeat, destruction, and debt—will not prevail against the church standing upon God's revealed truth (Matthew 16:18). For some time, far too many Christians in America have allowed hell's gates to prevail while they sit in church. Now is the time for us to waken from slumber, to confront the culture, and to help restore freedom's blessing! People of faith can and must protect our freedom and inspire strong, stable, effective, limited government power.

Jesus commissioned His followers to share the truth that sets people free and keeps them free. As we have seen, He said, "If the Son makes you free, you will be free indeed" (John 8:36). True freedom is living under the control of God, not under the control of any other power or influence.

When we compromise truth, we also compromise freedom and its blessings. Our nation is in the process of doing this, and we are marching toward the death of freedom and the destruction of meaningful national life.

In our nation we are presently following the course of decaying nations that we can observe around the world where intellectual, moral, and economic systems are collapsing. Some of the American leaders in power today are actually suggesting we follow other nations' tragic course.

I will gladly spend the rest of my life inspiring others to action. God is calling us to far more than religion. He is calling us to repentance; to a personal, intimate relationship with Him; and to the restoration of freedom's foundation. Religion is strong enough to make men hate one another, but it is not strong enough to make men love one another. God is calling us to a life filled with the power of transforming love and the boldness of New Testament believers to stand against the powers of this present darkness. A dying world is waiting for the release of the river of life that flows freely from the lives of yielded believers.

Living under God's control allows us not only to enjoy the privileges of freedom but also to protect them.

When God rules in individual lives, sound principles will prevail in our land. Leaders will no longer be chosen because of personality, party affiliation, or skillful communication. They will be chosen because of their commitment to God-given principles necessary for the survival of true freedom.

May we as Christians and lovers of freedom stand together to protect it! We will either witness the glorious future of freedom or the tragedy of its funeral.

Chapter 12

THE RESTORATION OF FREEDOM

There is no real freedom apart from God and the acceptance of personal responsibility. There can be no effective government without responsible citizens living under moral order. If we do not live under control with the freedom Jesus offers to all captives, then we can never hope for our society to support and maintain the principles that enable freedom.

With an understanding of the importance of personal freedom, we may rightly ask the question, "What about national freedom?" It is my firm opinion we are in the process of actually losing our national freedom, along with the opportunity it offers. It is my prayer that all believers will learn that we must live to protect what others died to provide. We are in the process of forfeiting the freedom our founders established—a freedom built on moral absolutes and a strong, but limited, government.

God has called me to pray for a spiritual awakening to bring about national repentance, sound thinking, and the restoration of freedom. Freedom is truth. Truth is the Word of God. Truth is the Bible. Truth is Jesus Christ. Apart from God's truth, God's Word, there is no freedom. Francis Scott Key wrote "The Star Spangled Banner" during the white heat of battle. When the firing finally stopped, Key said he strained to see if the flag was still there.[1] Today I find myself waking every day and looking to see if freedom is still here. My dear friends, we must not lose freedom.

We can maintain our freedom only by the eternal vigilance that has always been its price. Our republic was not established by cowards, and cowards will not preserve it. America will be the land of the free only as long as it is the home of the brave. America is a republic ruled by a constitution. We are not a democracy. A democracy is ruled by the majority. We are a republic. We are ruled by a constitution. We are not a monarchy, but we soon may be in anarchy.

Contrary to popular opinion, the American founders believed that everyone has a general knowledge of natural moral law and divine providence. From the heavens above to the conscience within, the world points to its Creator. That's why unbelievers still innately know that murder is wrong, injustice is immoral, and basic human rights are inalienable. We can see enough truth "through what has been made" so that we can be held accountable for our actions (Romans 1:20).

The existence of a Creator and a natural law are obvious truths. This is why in the Declaration of Independence the founders appealed to the "Laws of Nature and Nature's God," while purposely avoiding the establishment of a state religion. Even the Supreme Court, which hasn't always respected this part of our history, reiterated these points as recently as 1984, stating, "We are a religious people whose institutions presuppose a Supreme Being."[2]

Progressivism attempts to deny that God and morality can be known. It hides both of these truths in the closet of private religious faith. This has created the polar opposite of what our founders intended. We must reverse this trend and defend the truth that we can know moral truth, upon which we can build a just government. We must correct the false notion that faith demands theocracy and defend the freedom of believers to apply their faith to current issues.

We can be the guardians, the gatekeepers, the restorers of the foundation, and the wall builders maintaining our precious liberty. "Do not let your heart be troubled" (John 14:1). Keep the faith. Fight the fight as a good soldier of the Lord Jesus Christ with the whole armor of God and the sword of the Spirit. Don't bend and don't bow before the godless influences of this world, and you will not be crushed and enslaved by the powers in this present world!

We can maintain our freedom only by the eternal vigilance that has always been its price.

It's a myth that faith in the public square imperils freedom. In the past, some Christians have persecuted others, including fellow Christians. But they were violating the spirit and content of their faith in doing so. While not every religious belief is friendly to freedom, the basic tenets of the Judeo-Christian tradition reinforce political, economic, and religious freedom. We owe our American freedoms, in large part, to this tradition. Our faith is where we get our belief that individuals have equal value. It's also where we get the idea of sin, which inspired the founders to establish a limited government and a separation of powers.

Faith encourages the virtues that help sustain the free society. Edmund Burke, an Irishman who served in the British House of Commons, supported the American Revolution. A few years later, he opposed the French Revolution. Why did he support one, but not the other? The primary reason was because he understood the inherent danger in "liberty without wisdom and without virtue."[3]

We can help restore America and freedom. It will not be easy, but together, and with God's help, it can be done.

It is not too late for America. A righteous remnant remains. But we must return to the absolutes upon which our nation was founded before Independence Day becomes another meaningless holiday and freedom a forgotten notion of the past. The true church committed to Christ must arise and shine and lead the way out of this present darkness, proclaiming God's liberating truth in love, or America will soon join the ash heap of fallen nations.

Rather than surrender by withdrawing from public debate, we need to engage it in new ways. We must be able to defend our core principles clearly, directly, and compassionately. We need to explain how they relate to current issues and be consistent in our application of them.

America's decline is not inevitable, and we, as believers, have the solutions. Foundational principles established our freedom, and they can prolong it. Let us advocate them, live them, and elect those who hold to them.

Finally, may we never cease praying about all of our concerns. We can help restore America and freedom. It will not be easy, but together, and with God's help, it can be done. This is the greatest hour for people of faith to become a guiding light for our nation and our world.

PART

FOUR

EVIL MUST BE FOUGHT

In *Strive for Freedom*, Martin Luther King Jr. observed, "He who passively accepts evil is as much involved in it as he who helps to perpetrate it. He who accepts evil without protesting against it is really cooperating with it."[1]

The horrific terrorist attacks on 9/11, at the Boston Marathon, at the Christmas party in San Bernardino, and countless others are all clear demonstrations of undeniable evil. The mindless, heartless devastation and injury of innocent people reveals evil's intended end: destruction of life. Evil is evident by its disregard of everything meaningful, valuable, and important to life, peace, and security. Even those who doubt or deny the existence of God seem to acknowledge there is an undeniable force of evil present in this world, though many blame God for those who defy God in their evil actions.

The world faces an insidious enemy in radical Islamic

terrorism. It is far bigger than any one of its expressions such as al-Qaeda, Boko Haram, or the Islamic State. It does not reside solely in Islamic extremes, as evidenced in the atheistic massacres under Stalin and Mao during the twentieth century. Regardless of how it manifests, unrestrained evil is the enemy of all free societies.

God's Word challenges every believer to stand boldly, suited up in the armor of God, resisting evil's influence on every front. Evil will not be destroyed on this earth, but it can be defeated with wisdom from God.

Chapter 13
THE FACE OF EVIL

The man in black hid behind a balaclava as he pronounced a death sentence over journalist James Foley, brutally sawing off the American's head while cameras captured the horror. A month later, the hellish scene was repeated as another American, Steven Sotloff, met the same fate, with that same masked man presiding over the atrocity. The killer was Mohammed Emwazi, known as "Jihadi John" because of his British accent. He would also slay others, including British aid workers Alan Henning and David Haines, before being hunted down and eliminated in a drone strike. His identity was a source of much speculation when he first appeared in the snuff videos, but even before naming him, the world knew the face that lurked behind the mask. It was the face of evil.[1]

American leadership appears incapable of properly and effectively confronting evil. President Obama seems bewildered—

which is defined as "completely puzzled or confused, taken aback."[2] Like cancer and other deadly diseases, evil looks for a place of vulnerability, attacking areas of weakness, destroying that which is precious and all expressions of meaningful life. Evil is the enemy of faith, freedom, and peace. People of faith should pray for the courage and wisdom to face evil and thank God when lawbreakers, terrorists, and murderers are stopped.

God's Word is clear that we are to pray for our leaders (1 Timothy 2:1–2). They are given authority to punish the wicked while protecting the innocent. The Scriptures reveal that this authority must use "the sword" to stop evil attacks on guiltless people (Romans 13:3–4). Force, even if deadly, can be justified.

Every American should be deeply concerned when our nation's leader seems unable to recognize, identify, or call the enemy by its name. How could a medical doctor effectively deal with any destructive disease he cannot or refuses to properly identify? We who love freedom desperately need the immediate intervention and wisdom of divine providence. Our inability to clearly recognize and effectively deal with this very real enemy has paved the way for assaults right here in the "land of the free." We still possess brave men and women who stand ready to fight if they have a commander in chief who would effectively lead.

George Washington Carver, a great scientist, educator, and inventor, encouraged a friend by writing, "Keep your hand in that of the Master, walk daily by His side, so that you may lead others into the realms of true happiness, where a religion of hate (which poisons both body and soul) will be unknown, having in its place the 'Golden Rule' way, which is the 'Jesus Way' of life, will reign supreme."[3]

The earth was not designed by God to be the devil's playground. Never doubt Lucifer's intent to take it over, control it, and ultimately destroy it. God did not leave us here as His witnesses to live in defeat or defeated by the schemes of the devil. Hear the call of God! Become the witnesses He commissioned and set you aside to be. We must win hearts and minds to Christ even while seeking to win elections by putting people in office who have a biblical, God-centered worldview. If not, we will have given the enemy the reins and control of our children's future.

Relativism in our society today purposely blurs the distinctions between good and evil. But horrific actions, as we now routinely witness, snap us to attention and bring into stark focus the great chasm between right and wrong, righteousness and wickedness, good and evil. The reign of terror by the Islamic State brings us reports of men, women, and children being tortured, enslaved, crucified, and beheaded. It has even reached into our own neighborhoods. It is no longer a problem of the Middle East, Africa, or even Europe. It is here among us.

Hear the call of God! Become the witnesses He commissioned and set you aside to be.

If we lose the freedom that Americans appreciate and that we have been blessed to enjoy and share, it will be because Christians, church leaders, pastors, and priests did not find common ground to declare, demonstrate, and defend the truth that makes us free. The Great Commandment will have been ignored by those who profess to know God. The command to love Him with all our heart and love our neighbors will have been cast aside. The essential laws of nature and nature's God are being trampled underfoot because believers have failed to effectively be salt and light. We see innocent life destroyed in the womb, marriage redefined, and biblical morality ridiculed. It is imperative that those who love God and others find common ground to stand upon while declaring freedom's essential principles.

Our Father in heaven cares deeply for His family, and He offers security and protection from the deadly assault of enemies. Jesus, the Great Shepherd, will not rest with ninety-nine sheep in the safety of the fold but will diligently seek that one lost, vulnerable sheep (Luke 15:3–7). It is the will of Almighty God for every pastor, priest, and church member to diligently protect vulnerable people from the destroyer of life. Call for prayer on behalf of those threatened, and ask God for wisdom to build walls of protection and destroy evil's deadly intent.

Chapter 14

CONFRONTING EVIL

Today's enemies of life cannot always be as readily identified or eliminated as a single maniacal dictator, such as Adolph Hitler. There are untold numbers of demented "Hitlers" all over the world and even in our own midst. These terrorists are suicidal and murderous, willing to die in order to take out ten people or ten million. Their targets range from concert venues to office parties; from five-star restaurants to fast-food outlets; from the heart of Jerusalem to the heart of America.

Some terrorists will be very impatient, striking out in ineffective, poorly planned attacks. Others will be calculating enough to lease space in a high-rise building and deliver their weapon, perhaps even with nuclear capability, in a briefcase hidden under a rented desk after they are long gone. Hundreds of potential scenarios exist, and there is not enough military might to completely defeat or control this enemy. Supernatural wisdom and direction is our only hope.

The Pew Research Center reports that 89 percent of Americans believe in God.[1] Americans must meet this higher power. We must know the mind, will, and way of the one true God, because it is only through Him that we can find control and security.

Every great society has had to take evil into account. Decisive, principled action has been the only proven remedy to the problem of evil. Our nation's leaders must have the heart, courage, and humility to lead us without the fear of people and their opinions. Decisions must be guided by the absolute, unshakable principles upon which freedom was established and will safely stand.

The principles upon which our nation was established—ideas such as justice, peace, responsibility, and sacrifice—are our only safeguards. Those nations and individuals throughout the world who fail to understand these principles will never willingly make the sacrifices necessary to ensure freedom's survival. While everyone should rightly rejoice over victories such as the abolition of slavery, we should all weep over the possibility of Americans witnessing the abolition of liberty. If freedom is to survive, we must reengage the irrefutable absolutes to govern our lives and our society. Christians must steadfastly resist the forces of evil while offering comfort and counsel to those hurt by it.

President Reagan had the frankness and vigor to stand up against the Soviet threat. In our times of prayer together, he sought wisdom from above. He believed the verse I shared with him concerning security: "The shields of the earth belong to God" (Psalm 47:9). Reagan found the courage to convert retreat into advance and demand that the Soviets "tear down this wall" in Berlin[2] because he knew that the forces of good would eventually overcome the cruel and oppressive forces of evil. Backed by military superiority, America and the free world presented a better idea than Marxism. Ultimately, only a better idea can prevail over flawed ideology.

Our national, local, and church leaders must understand this truth today. We must recognize the depths of hatred and malevolence behind terrorist activities here at home and around the world. Good must ultimately triumph over evil. We must not fear evil; we must face it without spurning God's wisdom but embracing it. Our nation needs God-given insight, power, protection, direction, and wisdom at this critical moment in human history. There is no quick solution to the challenges we now face. The evil of terrorism will not soon go away. Only those who are strong, principled, and willing to sacrifice will endure and overcome. To face the evil that murders the innocent, frightens the weak, and enslaves the willing, we must reach higher, seek wisdom, and stand strong.

Christians must steadfastly resist the forces of evil while offering comfort and counsel to those hurt by it.

While Americans and freedom-loving people around the world openly express their horror at the heartless destruction of the innocent, should we not examine our own hearts as a people? Our great nation has silently allowed the termination of more than fifty million innocent lives in the wombs of their mothers.[3] Hitler murdered over eleven million people in the Holocaust, and Stalin almost twenty million. America has doubled that, and the casualties are still mounting.

As the trial of abortionist Kermit Gosnell quietly unfolded in 2013, the media was anxious to ignore it. His unconscionable taking of life puts the most murderous criminals to shame. The charges included the death of Karnamaya Mongar, a forty-one-year-old mother, and seven babies born alive and then cruelly put to death.[4] The media ran from this spectacular trial because it revealed the truth about their sacred "right" of abortion.

As the prophet Haggai implored the people, "Consider your ways!" (1:5, 7). While seeking protection from terrorism and other forms of evil, we must diligently seek God's divine enabling to recognize it in our own hearts and turn away from it. We must cease moving away from the hedge of protection offered by God's eternal Word and stop allowing principled walls of absolute truth to be torn down.

In his first inaugural address, Abraham Lincoln said, "Intelligence, patriotism, Christianity, and a firm reliance on Him, who has never yet forsaken this favored land, are still competent to adjust, in the best way, all our present difficulty."[5]

Sadly, these four things have evaporated in many people's hearts and minds. Voters are ill-informed and easily duped. Students are being taught to despise their country. God is not quietly rejected but openly mocked. People depend on government for what only God can provide. Our crumbling foundation must be restored if we expect to stand safely with the protection our founders recognized, appreciated, and depended upon: divine providence.

Chapter 15

SUBTLE EVILS

merica and the free world will always be safer when evildoers and evil deeds are properly handled. People of faith should pray for justice to be done and thank God when lawbreakers and murderers are stopped. I am indeed grateful Osama bin Laden was taken out through the united efforts of the intelligence agencies, President Obama, and his Security Council—and especially through the training, commitment, skill, and personal sacrifice on the part of our Special Forces.

While terrorism is an obvious evil, less blatant evils also exist. The only way these issues can be properly dealt with is through the same dedication, determination, and unity that exposed terror's figurehead and eliminated him.

God the Father revealed Himself in what He created (Romans 1:20). In our own bodies we can study the white blood cells resisting evil bacteria and battling for our health by identifying, isolating, and eliminating them. Whenever a germ or infection enters the body, the white blood cells snap to attention and race toward the scene. These cells are continually on the lookout for any sign of disease. When a malevolent presence appears, the white blood cells have a variety of ways by which they can attack. Lymphocytes produce protective antibodies that will overpower a virus. Neutrophils will surround and devour bacteria. In the same way, we must all together deal forcefully with evil. When the necessary response of healthy cells is adversely affected by a virus like HIV and they do not respond appropriately, overall health is damaged.

Many concerned Americans and Christians agree that there is a damaging viral worldview not only accepting bad moral, economic, and social practices but encouraging them. The long-term cost and damage inflicted through these beliefs and practices prove they have come from an evil root. Teaching people to place their hope and trust in something other than God is, in fact, the very essence of evil because it encourages idolatry, leading to misplaced trust, which ultimately damages everyone.

True believers fully understand that faith cannot be imposed, but neither should *no faith* in a supreme being be imposed by forcing people to violate their conscience and convictions. The practice by political leaders and the federal government of forsaking sound economic principles, and their manipulation of people by routinely taking their money, mismanaging it, wasting it, and driving our nation into unsustainable debt must be stopped or the general population will be led into subservient bondage. Unprincipled, misguided practices and abuses led to revolution, the founding of our great nation, and the establishment of the Constitution to protect us from such outrages. Today's unhealthy sense of entitlement and expectation, along with the demand to be cared for by the government while continually building hate for job- and wealth-creators, is, in fact, evil. If continued, it will create an animosity greater than racism. This form of class warfare cripples potential productivity and destroys any meaningful way to assist the poor, suffering, elderly, and helpless.

It is a waste of time to vent anger and frustration without offering valid solutions. Now is the time to pray without ceasing for God to bring His people together in heart-harmony and for our leaders to come and reason together with the same dedication, determination, and unity of purpose that exposed and eliminated the terrorist Osama bin Laden. The evil controlling him killed innocent people of all races and faiths. The practices supported by a present-day, damaging, collectivist, statist worldview promoted in our own nation kills futures, the economy, individual lives, and freedom itself.

My Christian friends, we are partly, if not largely, responsible for the present course of our nation because we allow it. We have tolerated the violation of

It is a waste of time to vent anger and frustration without offering valid solutions.

sound principles on the part of national leaders for many years. People claiming to have faith in God have been "at ease in Zion" (Amos 6:1)—complacent, indifferent, uninspired, uninformed, and uninvolved. It is time now for us to get on our knees in prayer and then stand up like a mighty army and help deliver the church and nation from evil. Pastors must join together to sound a clear alarm on the trumpet of truth so the people will prepare for the right battle in the right way and win by choosing righteousness. America's founders purchased and established our freedom with words, weapons, and their very lives. They died for it—surely we can live for it!

I am convinced if we make a firm commitment to stand and take action wisely, we can protect and preserve freedom with our voices and our votes. We still have the privilege and responsibility of choosing those who lead and the policies we support or oppose. We do have time if we recognize *now is the time* and return to God, restore freedom's foundation, and rebuild the walls of sound principles.

If you want to hear the absolute truth from a proven leader, a politician, an American president, listen to these powerful words from President Calvin Coolidge:

> If in a free republic a great government is the product of a great people, they will look to themselves rather than government for success. The destiny, the greatness of America lies around the hearthstone. If thrift and industry are taught there, and the example of self-sacrifice oft appears, if honor abide there, and high ideals, if there the building of fortune be subordinate to the building of character, America will live in security, rejoicing in an abundant prosperity and good government at home and in peace, respect, and confidence abroad. If these virtues be

absent then there is no power that can supply these blessings. Look well to the hearthstone, therein all hope for
America lies.[1]

Positive change starts with you and me. We need not look to
government, politicians, or other leaders for salvation, but only
to God. Our hope comes from Him. Our strength multiplies
when we come together in submission to Him. In the days of the
Israelites, God promised victory over their enemies as "five of
you will chase a hundred, and a hundred of you will chase ten
thousand, and your enemies will fall" (Leviticus 26:8). Later, the
converse was true when they rebelled against God and were defeated (Deuteronomy 32:30). It's only when God's people submit
to Him and come together that evil in all forms can be driven
from our land.

Chapter 16

GOD'S ANSWER TO EVIL

Satan is the author and instigator of all evil. He is the very personification of it. Even those who doubt or deny God cannot deny there is an obvious force of evil present in our world. Jesus said Satan is the father of all lies and, above all, a thief and murderer. He seeks to destroy life—every precious aspect of it. When he is in control, he continually manifests despicable, unimaginable acts defying all logic.

We are right to abhor unspeakable brutality and murder of the innocent and the helpless. Such was the case in December 2014 when schoolchildren and their adult supervisors were senselessly murdered in Newtown, Connecticut. The twenty-year-old lone gunman was delusional, paranoid, and deranged, but it was more than just that—it was demonic. No, the devil didn't make him do it. The murderer made a horrible choice.

Such is the case when resistance and clear-mindedness on

anyone's part have been compromised and diminished. Many things can negatively impact our spiritual and mental condition to some degree: addiction to alcohol or drugs, damaging emotions such as bitterness or envy, emotional or physical exhaustion. It can even be the result of self-intoxication, as with Herod at the time of Christ's birth. He ordered the murder of all little boys under two years old in Bethlehem (Matthew 2:16). Satanic? Yes. Demonic? Yes. Even so, it was Herod's choice to act on his evil schemes.

In the fatherless home and the dysfunctional community I grew up in, you cannot imagine the suggestions other kids made to me, along with the fiery darts (horrific suggestions) Satan fired my way. I was vulnerable; but thanks be to God, praying Christians, a pastor and his wife who never forgot the boy they cared for during the first few years of my life, and then the witness of committed Christian teenagers led me to Christ. I am convinced that the prayers of others (even before my conversion to Christ) helped prevent me from giving in to violent impulses, especially when my alcoholic father threatened to take my life. Sadly, some choose to give in to their anger and act out in unimaginable ways.

Jesus is the answer. He was my answer, and He is the sole answer for those devastated by manifestations of evil. Only a great God and a loving heavenly Father can give the ultimate comfort wanted and needed by the people of Newtown, Paris, San Bernardino, Fort Hood, and every community victimized by those who commit evil acts. Caring neighbors, friends, and other Christians will seek to lighten their load and brighten their future. Jesus is the only way to overcome evil and the evil one.

He alone can direct our steps and help us build wise, secure walls of protection.

God's Word should be our hedge of security. He wants His Word to be written in our hearts, not just carried in our hands. He wants His Word to carry and lead us and, as Paul said, write letters in the hearts of other people's lives as a result of our consistent Christian testimony (2 Corinthians 3:2–3).

Believers must demonstrate the resurrection life He offers each day. Jesus came to overcome the evil one and to give us the ability to be delivered from that despicable, damaging influence. We live only because Christ was born, was crucified, rose from the dead, and now lives. May others see Jesus living in us.

Jesus is the only way to overcome evil and the evil one. He alone can direct our steps and help us build wise, secure walls of protection.

Thirty years ago when I experienced a marvelous deliverance from the power of demonic assault due to spiritual burnout and physical exhaustion, I was undoubtedly vulnerable. During the time following my deliverance, God clearly revealed that in the last days evil would wax worse. Satan's nature will be more obviously manifested than at any time in history with indescribable, unfathomable, despicable acts of evil.

But the converse of that is also true. The church (true Christians—fully devoted followers of Christ) will become more like Jesus than in any time in history. Satan will be destroyed and evil demolished forever, but until then, believers must stand suited up in the whole armor of God, resisting evil on every front. We can be forever triumphant by snatching victory from the jaws of defeat when we allow the love, hope, and peace of Christ to prevail.

Jesus is God's answer to man's weakness and evil's intention. His story can become our story. Jesus took this broken, fatherless, and impoverished boy and delivered me from destruction and the intentions of the evil one. He will do the same for all who receive Him and follow Him with their whole heart. Jesus is the light that pierces the darkness. He offers strength beyond ourselves and grants us the grace and ability to share the hope, joy, and peace that only He can give in the face of the most challenging possible circumstances. Just as the shepherds and wise men followed the light of the star of Bethlehem, we must follow the light of the forever bright and morning star—Jesus!

PART
FIVE

LAWS MUST BE JUST

Our nation was birthed by a move of Almighty God, and the result was a spiritual awakening and a heart hunger for religious freedom. We must have a move of God like this to avoid the potential riotous activity of people stirred by charismatic communicators who are misguided and, in the guise of concern, are fueling the fires of riotous, destructive acts. We are observing a potential powder keg of emotion that only divine providence can quell.

Jesus told His followers there are definite standards by which we measure our lives, and we must understand righteousness is far more than just keeping the rules. It is allowing the important truths He shared to be written first in our hearts and then demonstrated through our lives, becoming a clear testimony revealed for all to witness. The light that He is and we are to be not only exposes error and irresponsible actions but also guides us in the way we are to go, making corrections and revealing how we can love and assist our neighbors even when they boldly declare to be our enemies.

We must never back down in the face of opposition and lawlessness. The Scripture makes it clear if we are captivated by God, we will not be intimidated because "perfect love casts out fear" (1 John 4:18). This is no time for timidity or passivity. As Christians, we are responsible to be salt and light, standing and resisting the fury of hell while loving those adversely influenced by it. In America, we have been given both the privilege and responsibility of choosing wise leaders who will pass and enforce laws consistent with time-proven principles.

Chapter 17

KNOW JUSTICE, KNOW PEACE

We hear the chant, "No Justice, No Peace," but we seem not to know the definition of either concept. In a world embracing relativism, one person's justice can be another man's crime. We need to return to some foundational truths before we can ever hope to achieve any kind of justice and foster a lasting peace.

Even before the birth of our nation, George Washington, as commander in chief of the Continental Army, wrote a letter on June 8, 1783, to address major issues facing the people at the end of the Revolutionary War. He closed it by urging all citizens "to do Justice, to love mercy, and to demean ourselves with that Charity, humility and pacific temper of mind, which were the Characteristicks [sic] of the Divine Author of our blessed Religion, and without an humble imitation of whose example in these things, we can never hope to be a happy Nation."[1]

These ideas—justice, mercy, charity, humility, self-restraint, religion, and happiness—are not detached. The ouster of God, the lack of self-control, the celebration of pride, and the disinterest in charity have led to a larger segment of unmerciful and unhappy people. It's no wonder that a clear sense of justice cannot be found in this fog of self-centeredness.

Our second president, John Adams, pointed to God as the source of our sense of justice, protection, blessings, and freedom by closing his inaugural address with this exhortation: "And may that Being who is supreme over all, the Patron of Order, the Fountain of Justice, and the Protector in all ages of the world of virtuous liberty, continue His blessing upon this nation and its Government and give it all possible success and duration consistent with the ends of His providence."[2]

A month before the end of the Civil War, in which the great injustice of slavery was undone, President Lincoln closed his second inaugural address with these famous words: "With malice toward none; with charity for all; with firmness in the right, as God gives us to see the right, let us strive on to finish the work we are in; to bind up the nation's wounds; to care for him who shall have borne the battle, and for his widow, and his orphan—to do all which may achieve and cherish a just, and a lasting peace, among ourselves, and with all nations."[3]

Perhaps more than any other factor, peace and justice go hand in hand. Our loss of divine wisdom has led to an inability to discern true justice, which has led to a loss of internal peace, which often spills into the streets as violence. As a nation, we must once again learn to recognize the invisible hand of God and turn to divine providence for guidance. The civil unrest in cities around the country, the contention in the halls of leadership, the efforts to divide "one nation under God" into "us against them," the shameful lack of proper stewardship, and a whole host of other social, political, and economic plagues all trace their roots back to one thing: a disregard for the divine.

Perhaps more than any other factor, peace and justice go hand in hand.

It would be easy to get discouraged or cynical. Cursing the darkness is always easier than sharing the light. But our Lord is patient. Like the father of the prodigal, He waits with open arms for us to return to His wisdom, protection, and blessings. If we will do that, we will once again discover how to live just and peaceful lives.

Chapter 18

THE PARABLE OF THE SCHOOL ZONE

To help you understand the importance of Christians' influence on our country, let me tell you a fictitious story I call "the parable of the school zone."

A few blocks from our subdivision there was an elementary school. We had a well-posted school zone with flashing yellow lights, requiring twenty miles an hour and no cell phones. Almost every day I observed loving parents and precious little children when I drove through the zone.

According to some relativist pundits, however, we must not expect laws to be consistently enforced because speed limits shouldn't have been there in the first place since there are no absolutes. From the religious came these assertions: "Everyone knows we are living in the last days and lawlessness will increase. Evil men will get worse and worse, since bad trees can never produce good fruit. There is no need to expect those living in open rebellion to any absolute laws to respect school zones." Other opinions included "Everyone should have enough common sense to see that the world is going to hell in a handbasket anyway" and "What will be, will be" and "It is what it is."

Many churchgoers seemed convinced the only kingdom that really matters to God is the future kingdom when all this evil stuff will be removed. Then there will be no challenges, no mountains, no valleys, no need to get suited up in any armor since there will be nothing to resist—all will be well. Jesus was simply being gracious and perhaps facetious when He instructed His disciples during the Sermon on the Mount to pray for the will of God the Father to be done on earth as it is in heaven. Surely He knew the only way this could possibly happen is for Him to hurry up and come get us because very little realistic difference can be made on this rebellious planet called Earth. Since the increase of lawlessness was clearly predicted and prophesied, it would be a waste of time and energy attempting to keep all those people from driving fifty miles an hour in the posted school zone. Dedicated Christians would never want to be represented as political activists—God forbid! You know Jesus Himself said His followers were merely sheep in the midst of wolves. What lasting respect could you possibly hope for? Sure enough, because of indifference, it appeared the furious floods of evil were pouring over the walls too weak to resist.

Several weeks ago three elementary schoolchildren were

killed in one day. As the parents of a kindergarten girl wept at the scene, they cried out loud, "She was so happy to be going to school for the first time in her life. I don't think any little girl was ever more excited." A number of onlookers simply shook their heads and walked away. A third-grade boy was also killed and two others were injured. The grieving parents and friends lamented the tragedy of the children's future coming to such an awful and abrupt end.

One afternoon, as the children were leaving, a fifth-grade girl was hit and knocked more than twenty feet, dying instantly. Her brown eyes were fixed wide open in sudden, unexpected death. I actually heard one person say, "Oh well, she would probably have just grown up to face problems like so many girls living in this evil day. Perhaps this is the better way." I thought, *Dear God, what am I hearing and seeing?*

By the end of the month, thirty children had been killed and twenty-two more seriously injured. The next week a mother and her son were struck and killed together. The mother's hand was still tightly gripping her third-grade son's fingers. She had told her friend, "I'm going to go every step of the way to make sure my son gets to and from school safely." One bystander commented, "See, when lawlessness prevails, there is nothing we can do about it. Who are we to impose our values on other people? After all, who is going to determine right and wrong?"

Several people listening to the discussion asserted, "Just who do people think they are to set limits and determine how someone must drive? Everyone is free and capable of making his or her own choices. If people were smart, they would just keep their children at home. It would be best for kids to stay inside all day and never go out to play in the neighborhood because it is too dangerous with pedophiles lurking everywhere. Not even the city parks are safe anymore."

A few days later, a large group gathered not far from the school zone, and a discussion ensued. A sincere but misguided church member said, "Those of us who really know God and know about His kingdom understand that the people of this world are going to live irresponsibly, self-centeredly, and totally indifferent toward the well-being of others."

I said, "I thought the reason we have stop signs and yellow lights in school zones is to keep irresponsible people under control because of their lawless practices. I believe we are supposed to enforce our laws in order to protect responsible citizens, all people, and certainly the innocent."

Another person answered, "Yes, but you cannot expect the people who don't know God to care about other people."

I responded, "I thought that those of us in the kingdom were commissioned to help other people know how to be born into God's kingdom through faith in Christ and live responsibly caring about others."

Someone shouted, "Yes, but the Bible's references to the kingdom of God are all in the future!"

I answered, "But what about Jesus saying that the kingdom is near—it's at hand; it's right here, right now? It would seem to me that we all want to enforce the laws so that we keep all people, including those who are not in the kingdom, alive long enough that they might hear what it means to be born into God's kingdom.

Also it would seem wise to me if we kept laws in place that keep believers alive long enough and free enough to be able to openly share and reveal to everyone the kingdom of love and light. Knowing that good government must be built on sound principles, our founders established the Constitution to protect everyone's right to life, liberty, and the pursuit of happiness."

A voice shouted, "That's just foolish nonsense. You are lost in some religious fantasyland."

A few days later at the suggestion of a number of people, a relatively large group gathered at a community center nearby. I decided to attend and prayerfully listen. Quite a few people with some religious background and some regular church attendees expressed similar sentiments. "You know, this is a sign of the times proving that we really are living in the last days and evil men are getting worse and worse. They're ungrateful and selfish and no one really is seeking after God. As the Bible says, 'A leopard cannot change its spots.'"

A scholarly person spoke up. "Well, God never has expected anything from a fallen world. Things are happening exactly the way the Bible says they will."

Another church member said, "That's why we just keep hoping and praying that Jesus will come back soon and get us out of this mess!"

Another person with numerous academic credentials said, "Who do people think they are to tell someone how fast they can drive anyway? They have their rights. Everything is relative! You can't tell others how to live their lives. Parents should teach their kids to get out of the way or stay home!"

One person boldly spoke out. "Well, I know what I'm going to do. I'm not going to put up with it. I'll put a stop to it! I'm going to a local supply house and buy some concrete and during the wee hours of the morning I'm getting out there with my wheelbarrow and water and mixing it up. I will pour speed bumps that will take the undercarriage out of any car going too fast." He asked, "Would anyone like to join me?" (I knew I would, but I remained quiet and listened, curious about the reaction that would come from the others.)

The immediate response was, "I wouldn't dare go with you and I wouldn't suggest you do it. You let someone hit that bump and knock their front end out of alignment and you will be taken to court and sued for everything you've got."

Another person said, "You can't expect the courts to stand with you on behalf of those children. After all, the highest court in the land has made a decision not to protect the lives of the most helpless, innocent individuals in our nation—a baby in the womb of its mother."

Someone said, "See, that's what I mean. It's just a sign of the times!"

One person quietly said, "Isn't there an old saying somewhere that 'when the righteous rule, the people are happy,' or something like that?"

Someone with venomous anger in her voice said, "Who do you people think you are? Who is anyone to tell someone else what righteousness is? What unparalleled arrogance! Obviously you are uneducated."

"That's right. There's not anything we can do about it. What will be, will be."

Another person said, "Someday it will all be over; and the sooner, the better."

An apparent church member spoke out and said, "Well, all I know is it's well with my soul. I know where I'm going when it all comes to an end. I'm leaving now, because I'm going to Bible study and a prayer meeting." People began to file out with countenances ranging from anger and frustration to concern and confusion.

As I left the meeting, I was thinking, *I can't believe this is happening in America.* When I got home, I sat down and reflected on what I had heard. I knew I must do something and would never remain silent or allow the carnage to continue if I could possibly help stop it. As I meditated, a question Jesus once asked His disciples seemed very meaningful to me at that moment: "Will you also go away?" Right then I understood how well Jesus knew what it feels like to be totally alone. I knew, however, that didn't matter because He would never leave me or forsake me or anyone else committed to His will. God the Father did forsake Jesus on the cross so those who trust Him will never be forsaken or really alone.

I know to some this parable of the school zone seems far-fetched. But please pause for a moment and seriously consider the trends, decisions, and policies put in place by Congress and the courts in recent times as well as the lack of consistent enforcement of laws. When any nation fails to establish, practice, and enforce principles consistent with biblical truth, they suffer serious consequences. This applies not only to Israel, the UK, and the USA, but all nations desiring to live with any expression of peace on earth. All concerned Americans and believers must stand united with God in supernatural unity against the forces of evil because righteousness always exalts a nation and sin will always be a reproach to any people.

I am convinced truly committed followers of Jesus are people not only full of compassion but also of deep convictions and unwavering courage. We must love all those with different views and opinions, but I do not believe silence or lack of participation is positive. There is much we can do to effectively resist a spirit of lawlessness. When considering present trends and the extreme, destructive actions presented in this parable, I can't help but wonder if many professing Christians and Americans are guilty of foolish, fatalistic apathy. We can and must stand in the gap as Nehemiah did, rebuilding walls necessary for everyone's safety.

Chapter 19

THERE ARE ABSOLUTES

A lmost every daily newspaper and newscast reveals a blatant disregard of God's Word, eternal truth, and undeniable principles. Over the last few years, we have witnessed assaults on our First Amendment rights, which protect freedom of speech, religion, and the press from government interference. We have also seen evidence of deceptive cover-ups in the Benghazi attack, the IRS targeting conservative nonprofits, and a disregard for the sanctity of life as exhibited by Dr. Kermit Gosnell's murders in his abortion clinic. Did you think you would ever witness such damaging practices, troubling trends, and apparent indifference?

The consequences of such actions are grave. The fact is, we do not actually break God's laws or scientific laws. We defy them, and doing so ultimately breaks us. Many Americans believe the only absolute is "there are no absolutes."

Our nation is drowning in a sea of relativism. As the brilliant contemporary philosopher Ravi Zacharias has pointed out while lecturing at Harvard, Oxford, and other major venues throughout the world, the pure relativist cuts off the branch on which he is sitting while telling you the branch cannot be severed. Nevertheless, relativism has gained currency in our society, greatly weakening our foundations.

Absolutes, however, do not change over time. They are not made to fit our circumstances. Instead, we must remake our thinking to conform to these truths. We must continually remind ourselves and others of the importance of moral and biblical absolutes.

The pressing realities we faced then are more urgent now. These are major problem areas, which should lead to focused, prayerful attention. We are in serious trouble for many reasons. National leaders lack the character to make wise decisions. Radical partisanship prevails at the expense of the people and our best interests. Comfort and economic prosperity have become more important than principled living. Compassion has been redefined from a personal touch to a take-and-distribute mentality that abdicates our God-given responsibilities and foolishly puts

We must continually remind ourselves and others of the importance of moral and biblical absolutes.

more power in the wrong hands. Our intelligence and protection agencies fail to safeguard our security because of bureaucratic tendencies to protect their turf and fret over public relations, thereby short-circuiting clear communication and cooperation.

Protecting innocence and the innocent has become an object of scorn. Justice has become a baseless, arbitrary thing.

We must reexamine some of these "first principles." They are not only the foundations of justice but the bedrock of a stable society.

1. *Evil is real.* Just look to Paris, San Bernardino, Boston, or scores of other marred cities where radical Islam has senselessly, randomly, and brutally struck. The ability to recognize and discern right and wrong is one of our most important responsibilities and requires wisdom that can only come from God.

2. *Ideas have consequences.* Every belief system will ultimately bear fruit—and the fruit will be consistent with the root from which it comes. It is time to take an honest look at the consequences of our ideas and practices. Have they led to a more just society?

3. *We are spiritual beings.* To deny the existence of God is to set our minds at war against our hearts. God exists, and He created us with the capacity to know His truth. As our founders expressed, God is not only essential to creating a system of justice but He is the source of true justice.

4. *The majority is not always right.* History—both secular and biblical—demonstrates that "popular" is not the same as "just." Democracy without responsible, principled, self-governing citizens will lead to *mob*ocracy. Laws must be based on something more firm than the blowing winds of public opinion.

5. *Truth withstands debate.* We can agree to disagree, but we must reaffirm our commitment to freedom of speech. Only then will truth be given a voice and the opportunity to transform society. Truth is much like a lion: turn it loose and it always defends itself.

6. *People matter most.* The apostle Paul said, "The whole Law is fulfilled in one word, in the statement, 'You shall love your neighbor as yourself'" (Galatians 5:14). The Bible has stern warnings for nations guilty of shedding innocent blood, whether through slavery, abortion, or other injustice. Every life is worth affirming, enabling, and protecting.

7. *Equality is not sameness.* God made no two people, no two fingerprints, and no two snowflakes the same. Difference and diversity are beautiful qualities. The cause of justice is made all the more essential by our differences in aptitude, motivation, and ability. Attempts to make all outcomes the same result in great injustice.

8. *If government doesn't serve, it will enslave.* We must be vigilant to keep the blessings of government within their proper bounds lest they come to dominate the whole of our lives. When society depends on government for sustenance, the people fall into bondage. Government has nothing it does not first take from its citizens.

9. *Truth has a source.* There are many other absolutes, and they have been revealed to us through the ages. Time-tested, historical principles can be found in the Bible, which is the Word of God. The principles of the New Testament as expressed through the life of Christ form the basis for just

living. Forsaking these principles for relative values creates the chaos we are witnessing today.

Long ago, the psalmist laid out the ultimate guide to wisdom, which leads to justice. We would benefit immensely if we would heed his counsel.

My son, if you will receive my words
And treasure my commandments within you,
Make your ear attentive to wisdom,
Incline your heart to understanding;
For if you cry for discernment,
Lift your voice for understanding;
If you seek her as silver
And search for her as for hidden treasures;
Then you will discern the fear of the LORD
And discover the knowledge of God.
For the LORD gives wisdom;
From His mouth come knowledge and understanding.
He stores up sound wisdom for the upright;
He is a shield to those who walk in integrity,
Guarding the paths of justice,
And He preserves the way of His godly ones.
Then you will discern righteousness and justice
And equity and every good course.
For wisdom will enter your heart
And knowledge will be pleasant to your soul;
Discretion will guard you,

Understanding will watch over you,

To deliver you from the way of evil,

From the man who speaks perverse things;

From those who leave the paths of uprightness

To walk in the ways of darkness;

Who delight in doing evil

And rejoice in the perversity of evil;

Whose paths are crooked,

And who are devious in their ways. (Proverbs 2:1–15)

Chapter 20

RAISING THE STANDARD

All of us have standards. We don't always live up to them, but we at least try. For Christians, the Bible sets the standard, even with the variations in interpretation. Others set the standard according to their individual ideas or inner compass. For all of us, federal and local governments set certain standards by which we are all expected to live. We call these "laws."

So what happens—or should happen—when we miss the standard? How should individuals and society as a whole respond to those who repeatedly violate the standards set by others? Is it ever right to impose one's standards upon another, especially when he or she may not accept the same standard? These are all important questions that must be explored in order for us to live together in a peaceful society.

So let's start with the purpose of standards. In the case of civil laws, these are, in theory, designed to help us live in harmony with others by protecting individual rights, punishing evil, and pursuing justice for all. Take a clear case such as murder. Our standard is that murder is wrong and, in some states, punishable by death. When someone commits murder, our nation's commitment to upholding the standard demands that the accused person be held for trial and, if found guilty, punished appropriately. The terms are decided by a jury of his or her peers, yet within predetermined boundaries.

What would happen if a jury suddenly decided that the predetermined boundaries didn't apply to them? What if they agreed that it was clearly first-degree murder but declared themselves no longer bound by law and, instead of convicting the murderer, appointed him as the local sheriff? In such a circumstance, the appropriate reaction would be one of outrage. The public outcry would not only be justified but entirely righteous. The very foundations of a civilized society would require that jury to conform to the standard. Yet many people live their lives as if constitutional and biblical standards should be adjusted to conform to their practices or preferences.

Granted, some standards need to be refined or even corrected. The Civil Rights Act of 1964, despite the opposing votes of Democrats in Congress, was a proper refinement of our nation's standards. But as a society, we must uphold standards and insist that individuals conform to them. We must never adjust the biblical or constitutional standard to accommodate anyone's moral failures or personal preferences.

Those who profess Christianity can also be guilty of attempting to adjust or change spiritual standards. Some do not wish to live by certain things in the Bible, so they ignore them or redefine them, often twisting the obvious meaning of Scripture to fit their ungodly desires. One of the clearest biblical references of people who altered the standard, which led to their demise, is the passage where Isaiah describes those who "call evil good, and good evil," "substitute darkness for light and light for darkness," and "substitute bitter for sweet and sweet for bitter" (Isaiah 5:20). Paul later noted how people "exchanged the truth of God for a lie" (Romans 1:25) in order to accommodate their rebellion. They not only lived out of control, but they lived under the control of unbridled appetites. Such is the case far too often today. As Christians, we must all hold fast to kingdom principles and point all parties and candidates to reliable standards.

We must never adjust the biblical or constitutional standard to accommodate anyone's moral failures or personal preferences.

Old Testament prophets consistently held up godly standards, calling the nation back to the solid foundation of truth. Jesus proclaimed that He was the ultimate standard for meaningful life. We must remember that we don't set the reliable standards; God does. If we confess Him as our God and Father, then we must live as clay in the hands of the Potter, allowing Him to shape us in Christlikeness.

In this world of clashing standards, we can only persuade people to consider our view when we learn to dialogue with as much grace as we have conviction. Most people can't have a healthy conversation about standards because they are controlled by the spirit of destruction and arrogance. As Christians, we know the spirit of destruction is the same as the spirit of deception. This is the enemy—the father of lies, the powers and principalities in the realm of darkness—seeking to destroy the essence of life by pitting us against one another and God's truth.

In political seasons, candidates don't simply attempt to persuade voters through reason or even outdebate the other candidate; they also try to destroy their opponent while manipulating and even bullying the electorate. The same is often true in theological circles. Influential Christian leaders not only attempt to expose a bad belief system but also seek to destroy those who have been influenced by it rather than trying to help people see the truth more clearly. Remember, it is God who gives us the spirit of understanding and revelation.

As Christians, we have to understand that we can enter into heated debates and discussions with the desire to prove a point, but never at the expense of destroying the other person. We must maintain a spirit of redemption in an attempt to help others see more clearly. This often takes time, but that's what love does. It gives us graciousness and patience, even when we are determined to effectively explain our position. Love is not cruel, mean, or hateful. There is a place for strong rebukes, but there is still an important line between the spirit of redemption and the spirit of destruction.

The church and those who profess to know Christ should become committed to righteous, biblical principles by first living them and then proclaiming them. We desperately need a spirit of redemption in our country to redeem everything valuable and restore everything important while rebuilding walls of security and protection. May God help us in these serious times. We must have serious discussions concerning important issues—life and death, freedom and bondage, prosperity and poverty, opportunity and responsibility. As believers, we must be controlled by the Spirit of God as we seek to share His truth and raise His standard of justice, all in the spirit of redemptive love.

PART

SIX

HONEST WEALTH
IS A GOOD THING

We must not misinterpret God's command to "be fruitful and multiply" (Genesis 1:28) as simply having children. That is critically important, but we also should become fruitful with everything God has entrusted to our oversight. God commissioned Adam and Eve to care for the garden, just as farmers today must care for their fields, however fertile or challenging those fields may be. The faithful farmer must diligently seek to increase production in order to meet his own needs, the needs of his family, and hopefully the needs of others.

God told the farmers in the Old Testament to leave crops in the corners of their fields for the poor to gather (Leviticus 19:9–10). That is a great lesson, though often overlooked. As important as it is to give to the poor, it is equally important to encourage those in need to put forth effort to meet their own needs. Under God's law, needy people had to come to the field and pick up what was left for them. There was effort, even work, involved.

Today's entitlement and welfare programs often sustain people in their addictions, enable involvement in gangs, and encourage idleness as people learn to simply wait for their expected check. Welfare recipients often resent those who are rich even though it is only because of their work that welfare exists. Simultaneously, because the system has been so abused, those who produce wealth often resent the welfare state, even though they favor the idea of a safety net for those genuinely in need.

In a sense, many Americans live in the same type of bondage Israel experienced when they were taught to depend upon Pharaoh, who made slaves out of the people because they trusted in the wrong source. We can avoid their fate by turning our eyes back to the only Source of our hope, Jesus Christ.

Chapter 21

AMERICA AND THE POOR

Jesus loved and cared deeply for the poor. Both the Old and New Testaments are filled with the commandments of God to care for the poor, for widows, and for orphans. The parable of the good Samaritan (Luke 10:30–37) is a perfect example of an appropriate expression of compassion. Both the priest and Levite walked by and paid no attention to the one in obvious need. Religious traditionalists too often neglect the direct commands of God and follow their own lifeless, loveless traditions. Assisting the poor is a love expressed directly to the Lord. What greater source of inspiration could be found to encourage us to notice and help those who suffer? When we minister to the poor, we are also serving Jesus.

Betty and I, our family, and the supporters of LIFE Outreach have discovered indescribable joy and a sense of eternal accomplishment to the glory of God when we offer meaningful assistance to the poor and suffering around the world. God is well pleased, and His peace and His provision prevail in our lives even in the face of fierce challenges and obvious heartache.

One of the most beautiful memories of our daughter Robin, who went to be with Jesus three days after Christmas in 2012, occurred when we arrived at her first home in Tulsa, Oklahoma. As we drove up to her house, her children rushed to our car with little sandwich bags filled with money, smiling and shouting, "Mimi and Papaw, here is money we earned and saved to help feed hungry children!" What a blessing this was, and we give thanks to God for it.

Please hear my heart concerning our nation and the poor. America's poor and needy are being hurt and held back by bad policies and practices on the part of our own government. All manner of evil and liberal, even godless, causes are being encouraged and supported by what mainstream media and activists refer to as "social justice." This has proven to be a gross injustice to every American, and especially the poor.

What President Lyndon B. Johnson launched as a war on poverty has proven to be a war on the poor that actually keeps many not only poor but hopelessly enslaved as dependents with little or no confidence or meaningful ambition. The pitiful plight of the needy has made them the pawns of politicians who need their votes to retain their power. This practice is not only insane; it is cruel and will cripple America economically. Realistic chances to succeed, gain wealth, and generate a stable income will disappear. In the name of social justice, we are tolerating and even supporting horrible injustice.

Consider the destruction of the wicked cities of Sodom and Gomorrah. Unnatural sexual attraction and evil practices prevailed, but that is not why God destroyed Sodom and Gomorrah. Ezekiel 16:49–50 says, "Behold, this was the guilt of your sister Sodom: she and her daughters had arrogance, abundant food and careless ease, but she did not help the poor and needy. Thus they were haughty and committed abominations before Me. Therefore I removed them when I saw it."

America may not be destroyed with fire from above, but the raging fires of lust, greed, addiction, idolatry, and trusting in people rather than God and His truth will become our sources of destruction. Look what "We the People" have allowed to happen in our nation. Satisfaction with the success and wealth of personal prosperity has led far too many Americans to trust the blessings that freedom made possible while forsaking the truth and the living God who is necessary to set us free and keep us free.

We have allowed our government to collect excessive taxes, supposedly just on the rich, although the expenses reach down to every level of society through increased tax rates and higher prices on everything from gas and electricity to groceries and goods as well as property and travel. When we question the revenue generated through higher taxes, we are told that any tax reduction will hurt pregnant mothers, handicapped children, and of course the poor. Never mind the fact that money flows to bloated union bureaucrats, green energy companies (many of which have gone bankrupt), hardline Muslim groups in the Middle East and North Africa, and hundreds of other questionable or wasteful recipients. The false impression is that social justice is on the rise and the poor are better off than ever before.

Because of this deception, many Americans have begun overlooking their neighbors, just as the priest and Levite did in the parable of the good Samaritan. Meaningful assistance to the poor has diminished. The poor are now imprisoned by a sense of entitlement and have lost the vision to reach for their own success through personal determination.

Most Americans think that economic conservatives, political conservatives, and highly successful people do not care about the poor and needy. In most cases, this is not true. The responsibility for providing meaningful assistance to the needy must not be left to the government and misguided politicians. Motivated and capable citizens must prove they care by leading with compassionate action and demonstrating their concern by producing meaningful, positive results.

We must give people a hand *up*, not a hand *out*. This requires serious personal attention and involvement! Government programs must be managed by wise, caring overseers to prevent waste and to continue supporting only what proves to be effective. Those who pay most of the taxes must assume responsibility for ensuring that all hard-earned dollars are used wisely to produce the best results. We cannot hand off that responsibility or the responsibility for assisting the needy to those who continually prove they do neither well.

I continually thank God that, although I grew up poor, my single mother showed me the grace found in Christ that gives us the ability to forgive and not be controlled by bitterness or hate. I did not have to live poor, dependent, or defeated. My mother inspired me to read biographies about great Americans and leaders throughout history. She told me God could do anything if people trust Him and work hard. Even as a child, I never resented people who were better off than I was. I knew that if I wanted anything, I would have to go to work. I started working at age twelve, and I've never stopped. I am grateful I did not sit back with animosity toward others and wait for the state or a government agency to take care of me. I realized that I was not poor because other people were rich.

This is the same message Dr. Ben Carson heard from his own mother while he lived in poverty without a father in Detroit. Our backgrounds and our stories are similar.[1] With determination and faith in God, we were able to dig our way out of the mire of misery and depravity. Our lives are just two examples of what God, hard work, and true freedom make possible if only we believe and act.

Our nation will not be spared from catastrophic economic and moral collapse unless we turn to God and experience the necessary spiritual awakening. The collapse is imminent but by no means necessary. We can correct our course. God's challenge is the one that must be heeded. People who are considered rich (the top 10 percent), who pay 70 percent of the federal income tax, must recognize much of that money is not being used effectively. Their tax money is being wasted and used to support government programs that destroy the opportunity and freedom that enabled them to succeed. The government's ever-increasing entitlement programs are failing, so the wealth producers must do more than pay high taxes that will be terribly mismanaged—they must become personally involved in alleviating very real human suffering.

The successful can assist the poor by giving personal attention to their plight. Every American and certainly all who claim faith in God must become involved in establishing and supporting compassionate connections with the needy. First, we give ourselves totally to God, then we give from our money and time to help neighbors in need. Nothing is impossible for us to accomplish for the glory of God and benefit of others. We must stop making excuses, blaming others, and dismissing ourselves from personal responsibility and our divine assignment.

All who claim faith in God must become involved in establishing and supporting compassionate connections with the needy.

Determination, focus, and entrepreneurial diligence produce wealth and prosperity. Money in itself is not evil. It is necessary to be used as a blessing for us, our families, and others. It is "the *love* of money" that leads to "all sorts of evil" (1 Timothy 6:10). This misplaced love of wealth dims our vision, leading to blindness and spiritual deafness that will contribute to our downfall. It was likely the love of money, laziness, and lack of attention to the poor that paved the way for the moral decadence and wickedness rampant in Sodom and Gomorrah. This is now happening in America, our once-beautiful nation.

God is eager and able to correct us, save us, and use us to bless others as we express His love through compassionate assistance to those in need. Some, especially the rich, may find true repentance difficult, but with God all things are possible. It is God and God alone who can and will heal our land when we humble ourselves, pray, seek His face, and turn from our wicked ways—which include the love of money, success, selfishness, prevailing indifference, idolatry, faithlessness, and dead religion.

We must repent and change our ways! Then God "will make up to you for the years that the swarming locust"—which, for America, is our foolish decisions—"has eaten" (Joel 2:25).

Chapter 22

THOU SHALT NOT COVET

A merica's ongoing rebellion against the most basic tenets of God continues to progress with each election cycle. The current emphasis seems to celebrate an attitude specifically denounced in the Old Testament's Tenth Commandment:

> You shall not covet your neighbor's house; you shall not covet your neighbor's wife or his male servant or his female servant or his ox or his donkey or anything that belongs to your neighbor. (Exodus 20:17)

Covetousness is also condemned by the apostle Paul in his letter to the Romans (7:7–12). But exactly how does one "covet"? The Hebrew idea conveys "desiring" and "being attracted to." The Greek denotes "lusting after." Coveting is not merely desiring a need to be satisfied, but it is a far more powerful impulse to possess an object, status, or person. Yet the sin lies not in the actual desire, but in the object of that desire.

Notice that the commandment does not forbid us to want a house, a spouse, employees, success, or prosperity. Instead, God tells us not to yearn for *our neighbor*'s house, spouse, or anything else. You can seek a spouse, but you are not to seek your neighbor's spouse.

The fact that God mentioned a house and other possessions in this commandment implies direct and distinct ownership. Your neighbor's donkey is not your donkey. It is his. He owns it. You can have your own donkey, but keep your hands (and your mind) off his. If there were no such thing as private and personal property, God would have given us the Nine Commandments.

Enter into this condemnation of covetousness the modern American idea of "fairness." Does your neighbor have a bigger house than you? That's not fair! Does your boss get a bigger paycheck? Not fair!

It could be pointed out that America itself is not fair by this measure. Just look south of the border to see a country where the "poor" in America instantly become middle class, if not rich. According to a 2011 report by The Heritage Foundation, 92 percent of America's "poor" have a microwave, 80 percent have air-conditioning, 66 percent have a DVD player and cable or satellite television, and nearly 75 percent have at least one car or truck. In addition, 96 percent of "poor" parents stated that their children never went hungry at any time during the year due to lack of money.[1] In any third-world nation, a person with these possessions and blessings would be undeniably rich.

This is not to minimize poverty by any measure but to point out that the constant stirring of envy and strife between the poor and the rich in America flies in the face of godliness. The resurging agitation of the so-called 99 percent against a highly selective group of one-percenters not only defies logic but fails the smell test as well. Ask yourself this: Would you rather occupy a tent in a public park or the corner office of a successful business? Would you rather your child grow up to be an angry protestor or Bill Gates? Or how about just having job security by being employed by a successful small-business owner or a stable corporation providing something others need or want?

The vast majority of Americans—and people of every nation—want a decent place to live with enough wealth to determine their own future. This means being free to succeed (and occasionally fail) in business without someone seizing their assets under the banner of "fairness." Behind that rhetoric lies nothing but envy and covetousness. Those controlled by covetousness do not want just to be left alone in their own house—they want your house or someone else's.

There are also those who seem to think that if everyone can't have something equally, then no one should have it at all. I certainly believe everyone should have the freedom to earn, achieve, gain, or purchase, but there will always be certain limitations. Limits should never be forced in place because of envy or greed.

This is clearly the strategy of liberals, progressives, and socialists. We are being told that the only remedy to high unemployment and a stagnant economy is to take someone else's wealth by force. The truth is that the solution can only be found through wealth creation. And herein lies the fundamental problem.

A large segment of society fails to understand the basic truth that prosperity, opportunity, and wealth are *created*, not simply shared. When a nation needs more jobs, they must be created, not taken from one and given to another. Wealth is not finite. There is not a limited pie that can only be cut into so many pieces. God has given us the ability to create more. Those who do not know God perpetuate the false notion that someone else has unfairly taken a bigger piece of the pie than he or she deserves. They do not recognize, or simply refuse to admit, that every one of us has the God-given ability to create our own "pie" and then share with others as we see fit. We need not covet our neighbor's; we only need to make our own. It is important to remember that people created in the image of God can create necessary resources. Mankind, not matter, is the ultimate resource.

> *A large segment of society fails to understand that prosperity, opportunity, and wealth are created, not simply shared.*

Furthermore, the notion that the rich have only gotten rich because they have taken from the poor cannot hold up under scrutiny. Obviously there are the Bernie Madoffs of the world. There are thieves who have become rich (and more who remain poor), but they are the exception, not the rule. I do not believe that Steve Jobs, Oprah Winfrey, Michael Jordan, Sam Walton, Mark Zuckerberg, and most wealthy Americans cheated the masses in order to gain. Instead, they invented, entertained, engineered, and innovated.

This is wealth creation, and it's something we can all do,

though not to identical levels. Some people will succeed with a little; others will succeed with a lot. The point is that all of us must remain faithful with what we have, acquire any wealth honestly and honorably, and use it for good. If we would each do that, then we wouldn't care that someone else might have bigger, better, or more.

Chapter 23

JESUS STARTED WITH INEQUALITY

'Ve always found Jesus's parable of the talents (a monetary unit) in Matthew 25 to be interesting and provocative. In this story the master gives three of his servants different amounts of money. He starts with income inequality! Then he goes on a journey, and when he returns, he examines what the three servants have accomplished with what they were given. The ones who created more wealth are called "good and faithful" (vv. 21, 23), while the one who returned the same amount he was given is characterized as "wicked" and "lazy" (v. 26). Those aren't my words; those are the words of Jesus. The third servant didn't squander or lose what his master gave him; he was simply not fruitful or productive with what was entrusted to him.

As one who cares deeply about those in every income bracket, and especially the poor, I want everyone to know the truths that will set them free to be productive. Much of the rhetoric we hear in America today creates division, strife, envy, and resentment. This is not of God and will continue to hinder our economic recovery.

Politicians and activists have been arguing for years that an "income gap" is not merely an economic fact or a social norm but also a moral defect.[1] Their answer, predictably, is government intervention. If this were a discussion of poverty, perhaps a stronger argument could be made, but it goes beyond that. It gets into the difference between an average middle-class family and a professional athlete or Hollywood celebrity. After all, there is a huge difference between living off of thousands of dollars and millions of dollars.

We should all be concerned about poverty, but even if poverty were eliminated, there would still be "income inequality" between people. Let's face it: some jobs just aren't going to receive the same salary. For example, a society will not pay the same amount for a janitor as they do for a doctor. Not to mention the fact that a single person has no real need to make as much as a family of four. Also overlooked in the discussion is the cost of living variation between regions. Ask a person in New York City how far $100,000 a year goes and his or her answer will be vastly different from someone in a rural Kansas town.

Jim Wallis, an activist minister and founder of *Sojourners* magazine, has gone beyond calling income inequality a moral problem by saying, "God hates inequality."[2] It is apparently, in his thinking, a theological problem. In response, my close friend and coworker Jay Richards wrote, "The Judeo-Christian tradition teaches that everyone is created in the image of God, and so all people, whatever their social status, should be treated with dignity and as equals before the law. There's a lot about greed in the Bible, but not a single passage of Scripture or traditional Judeo-Christian teaching suggests that *income* inequality, in itself, is a moral evil."[3]

So why is income inequality a concern, even among Christians? One reason is ignorance of the idea that *wealth is created*. Too many people have become convinced that wealth can only be shared, which often means stolen. If someone makes a million dollars a year, this line of thought goes, then it's only because another hundred people only make $50,000 a year. They think a company's CEO can only get a big Christmas bonus by underpaying his or her employees.

This thinking comes from a complete failure to understand a free-market economy. Would anyone accuse LeBron James of stealing from people who paid to watch him play basketball or bought apparel with his name on the logo? Of course not. He has made millions of dollars—far more than the vast majority of people in the entire world—by taking proper advantage of the free market. He first worked hard at a sport that people wanted to watch. He made himself valuable, and people eagerly gave up money to see him. He then licensed out his name and image to create demand for shoes, hoodies, and other merchandise. Nobody forced anyone to buy these items, and he never took anything from anyone. LeBron made his fortune through hard work, business acumen, and the free market. In the process, he created massive income inequality. I see no theological, moral, or societal problem in any of that. (LeBron has also started his own charity and has been involved in many good works to help others, which is admirable.)

Everyone has diverse skills, interests, and abilities. They are not all worth the same on an economic scale, nor should they be. Many people aren't even interested in making the same as everyone else. If a young single man loves the outdoors so much that he is content sleeping in a tent and guiding fishermen in remote Montana, even though he makes a fraction of the salary of a Wall Street banker or a Silicon Valley computer programmer, shouldn't he be able to do so? Leveling the payment field would not result in the fishing guide becoming rich; it would result in the banker and programmer becoming poor.

All Americans, and especially Christians, should be concerned about poverty. We should seek ways to help the poor and teach them how to help themselves. We should also go after those who abuse the free market, whether it's through cronyism, corruption, or any other dishonest means. But we should not buy into the lie that inequality is always a bad thing. Income inequality is necessary, natural, and largely benign.

Chapter 24

DON'T KILL THE GOOSE

One of the most familiar of Aesop's fables is "The Goose and the Golden Egg":

There was once a Countryman who possessed the most wonderful Goose you can imagine, for every day when he visited the nest, the Goose had laid a beautiful, glittering, golden egg.

The Countryman took the eggs to market and soon began to get rich. But it was not long before he grew impatient with the Goose because she gave him only a single golden egg a day. He was not getting rich fast enough.

Then one day, after he had finished counting his money, the idea came to him that he could get all the golden eggs at once by killing the Goose and cutting it open. But when the deed was done, not a single golden egg did he find, and his precious Goose was dead.[1]

In America what represents the golden goose in Aesop's famous fable? Our nation's "golden goose" are her citizens, created in the image of God, who today, because of the faith and wisdom of our nation's founders, live with the freedom to create, work hard, and prosper. America's liberty grants us both the privilege and responsibility to meet needs and challenges while pursuing our own dreams and assisting others in meaningful pursuits.

Our Creator and heavenly Father loves to see His children blessed and freely able to bless others. History reveals that when people no longer recognize God in the first place as the wise, overseeing Father, they forfeit their freedom through foolish idolatry, selfish indulgences, irresponsibility, and insensitivity to God and others. When we fail to love God and our neighbors, we will lose our freedom and watch our productivity diminish. The inability to produce wealth and prosperity not only robs us of our own blessing but also prevents us from being in a position to bless others.

The noose that kills the goose is excessive control by any power other than God and the effective oversight given by free and responsible people. In America, this noose is the overreaching and excessive control of an ever-expanding, all-consuming federal government and its bureaucracies, along with freedom-damaging regulations. Supported by the godless idea that the government can care for its citizens better than they can care for themselves and others, the noose is rapidly tightening and choking out the life and freedom that were handed to us by those who understood freedom, responsibility, and true prosperity. The excess and greed on the part of those who prosper, as well as the envy and covetousness of those who lack, are used to justify the federal noose being tightened, ultimately killing the goose that enabled us to be the most prosperous and benevolent nation in history. Never doubt that the father of lies is determined to steal, kill, and destroy (John 10:10).

We must remember that the same success and prosperity that consumes some people, leading them to be totally selfish, also enables those who have been blessed and prosper to assist the poor and needy. Those who work hard and succeed help fuel the economy by investing, creating business and opportunity, and producing the benefits derived from their consumerism. A person must have a measure of wealth and a level of prosperity to be able to purchase something they need or desire.

To use a simple example, whether a family has the means to buy one car for the whole family or a car for every member of their family, that family's purchase supports the production of automobiles. Whether one family owns four cars or four families each own one car, the purchase of those cars has still provided jobs for the labor force. If a person buys one house or perhaps more, the housing market is strengthened. If no one has the ability to make a purchase, then the economy is drastically weakened. There must be a labor force to produce what people need and entrepreneurs to create things people want. It is always best for purchases to be made by those who can afford to make the payments immediately or in a timely manner.

Never doubt that out-of-control people will lose their freedom to an out-of-control, all-consuming power. Truly free people will keep the Ten Commandments, including the first, "You shall have no other gods before Me" (Exodus 20:3) and the last, "You shall not covet" (v. 17). Put God first, work hard, and be productive, while encouraging everyone to assist others. We need to be committed and consecrated to God, followed by compassion and care for others. When this happens we will watch America's golden goose soar like an eagle and gratefully behold the manifest blessings of our God and Father. This will happen when we decide to put God and others before ourselves instead of foolishly assaulting the goose of opportunity.

Let me share a simple Bible lesson. The prodigal son received from his father his rightful inheritance and then proceeded to mismanage and waste it until he found himself in great want. The loving father waited eagerly for the son to come to his senses and return home, making things right. The prodigal returned home as a repentant son with a changed heart and the attitude of a humble, willing servant (Luke 15:11–32). Problem solved!

Put God first, work hard, and be productive, while encouraging everyone to assist others.

In no way did the wise father give that foolish son more money to waste after he ran out. No way! Our out-of-control government demands that we continue to give it more to mismanage without first coming to its senses and finding every possible way to reduce government spending. If you want to rapidly assist the tightening of the noose that will kill the goose, just give irresponsible leaders more of the American people's means to waste with mismanagement. Don't dare attempt to justify this wrongdoing by saying the money will be taken from someone else (like the rich, our children, and those yet to be born), and that will justify the foolishness. It will not! It is easy to overlook stealing when the money is not yours.

A free market is a golden goose. It is a blessing of God. We must not destroy it in our attempt to solve injustices. Doing so will not raise anyone up; it will only tear everyone down.

PART
SEVEN

SMALLER GOVERNMENT
MAKES BIGGER CITIZENS

The Old Testament reveals that God as Father wanted a family through which He could bless all the nations of the earth (Genesis 12:1–3). He chose the descendants of the twelve sons of Jacob, known as the Israelites. The wise will learn from their journey. Paul said that what happened to Israel was an example for us (1 Corinthians 10:6, 11).

When ancient Israel wandered into idolatrous foolishness, they ended up in oppression and bondage. Search the Scriptures and observe the progression from freedom to slavery, from prosperity to poverty. In Genesis, the Israelites sold themselves into Egyptian bondage. Even after the Lord led His people into the promised land, many rejected His rule and ended up oppressed until they repented and He freed them again (Nehemiah 9). Once

God restored their freedom and blessings, however, the cycle of rejection and oppression would start over again.

Perhaps the most incredible expression of this pattern came fairly early in the Israelites' experience. After Moses freed the nation from the cruel enslavement of Pharaoh, they found themselves in the desert between bondage and the promised land. They were on their way but hadn't yet arrived when many complained, "Would it not be better for us to return to Egypt?" (Numbers 14:3).

Such is the case with America. Birthed by those who were fleeing oppressive governments and longing for liberty, we are now asking, "Would it not be better to return to big government?"

Just as Pharaoh awaited the Israelites back in Egypt, ready and willing to enslave them once again, the spirit of Pharaoh awaits America to revert back to the oppression and government dependency that our forefathers fled. The question is, will we go?

Chapter 25

AMERICA'S NEW PHARAOH

America's Pharaoh is not a person or a political party. It is a power source other than God upon which people erroneously and foolishly depend—and even begin to worship. It replaces God, exalting an unprincipled, unbiblical worldview. The advocates and supporters of this system consistently assault absolute principles while rejecting revealed truth.

Those who disagree with the forces of this Pharaoh are demonized in every possible way. Question their views, statements, or policies, and you are branded a racist, misogynist, homophobe, Islamophobe, bigot, Bible-thumper, and on and on. If you don't cave to their every demand, you are called a hostage holder. If you insist on any financial accountability, you can be called an assassin, holding "a gun at the head of the American people."[1] If you support the ideal of marriage, you are chastised as a religious zealot, opposed to love, fairness, and equality. If you uphold the sanctity of human life, you are labeled anti-choice and a hater of women. If you allow your faith in Christ to affect your words, actions, and beliefs, you are compared to jihadists and declared an enemy of America.

Obviously I don't agree with these negative caricatures. I refuse to accept the lame, dishonest labels some media pundits, representatives, and politicians try to put on principled Americans. I will not bow down to any idol that people choose to laud as the all-provident source upon which people must learn to trust. There is no substitute for the true and living God—the Father and Creator of all life and the only way to freedom, both personally and nationally.

I will stand against the lies promoted and substituted for God's eternal, unshakable truth and the only foundation on which we can safely build our lives and futures. We are witnessing firsthand—up close and personal—the exaltation of an idol that cannot succeed, because it never has and never will. This idol is being presented as a substitute for God, who is the only real provider, true source, reliable overseer, and worthy Father. He alone is the way, the truth, and the life (John 14:6). Substitutes are not the true Father, not the source, and are certainly not the way, the truth, or the life.

We are witnessing the enemy, the father of lies, attempting to overthrow God and exalt a new Pharaoh, false kings, unreliable rulers, a federal monarchy, rotten policies, and terrible laws. Regarding the Patient Protection and Affordable Care Act of 2010 (the so-called Affordable Healthcare Act), we have been told that once Congress passed it as a law (or a tax—who knows?), it is not to be challenged. Of course, slavery was once the law. That didn't make it good, moral, or just. Prohibition was once the law. Should that law not have been overturned?

The vacuous logic of "it's the law, so it shouldn't be challenged" never would have allowed a woman to vote or extended civil rights to African Americans. If those unjust laws remained unchallenged, progress would not have been made. But under the spirit of the new Pharaoh, such things are not to be questioned.

We have awful laws and policies now being thrust—yes, forced—on the American people. They are not merely unprincipled, but they are also unbiblical, ineffective, and unsustainable. If you believe in proven principles and dislike bad practices and proven-to-fail policies, you are now painted and perceived as the enemy. Americans who care deeply about right and wrong are not trying to bring the government down—we are trying to bring it under control.

Call me any name you wish. Put any misrepresentation or so-called politically correct label on me, but I am declaring that America is being encouraged to believe and embrace lies. Not only are we pressured to cast aside our founders' principles, but we are asked to ignore or suppress God's Word and eternal truths. The federal government and deceived representatives are forcing legislation, policies, and practices on American citizens, demanding that our tax dollars—our resources that God has trusted to our care—be used to support worthless, godless, and damaging policies, programs, and laws. This insanity

Americans who care deeply about right and wrong are not trying to bring the government down—we are trying to bring it under control.

has to stop before we have no choice but to submit to the bondage of an out-of-control state.

Americans must come to our senses and reject this idolatry. We must refuse to bow to any false god or trust it as our source. Not Pharaoh, not Nebuchadnezzar, not Babylon, not Rome, not emperors, not kings, not monarchies, and not Washington or Uncle Sam. Only God!

Our federal government must be brought back under control to serve the people—not to force us into servitude. The government must once again be by the people, of the people, and for the people. It must never be presented as the all-provident God. It is not! We must vertically look up to God and horizontally reach out to one another in truth and love. This is the transforming power of the cross. Look up to God the Father in childlike trust, and reach out to our neighbors with compassionate love and meaningful assistance.

Now is the time to stand against the gates and forces of hell as faithful witnesses—ambassadors of truth—exalting God's Word and life in His kingdom today. Refuse to stay hidden, keeping His truth only in church buildings! Become the blood-bought, born-again body of believers, the church of the living God, a city on a hill that cannot and will not be hidden any longer! Failure to heed God's invitation to live in His shadow and shelter while following the Shepherd will lead to the loss of freedom we have been blessed to know, and then this freedom will vanish from this earth.

The Bible says, "The earth is the LORD's, and the fulness thereof" (Psalm 24:1 KJV). Believers must stop turning God's planet over to the deceiver and another Pharaoh. Let's reclaim the land that was established and built on freedom's promise.

Chapter 26

SMALL GOD, BIG GOVERNMENT

When God and spiritual life decrease in importance, government expands rapidly. The less we hear God's unadulterated Word, the duller our hearing.

The prophets who spoke to Israel said that the nation had eyes but could not see and they had ears but could not hear (Psalm 115:5–6; Isaiah 44:18; Jeremiah 6:10). Faith fails when God's Word, which is necessary to open our ears to hear, is not faithfully declared. The Word tunes our ears to hear clearly in the spiritual realm so that we can walk in the light of divine guidance. When we do not see and hear clearly, we will make poor choices concerning those who serve and are chosen to lead. The population begins to believe lies, and there is no more dangerous person than the deceiver who thinks he is telling the truth. Those who are deceived are most effective deceiving others. The prophet Jeremiah said to a nation facing similar problems as ours, "The LORD has rejected those in whom you trust, and you will not prosper with them" (Jeremiah 2:37).

Without the wisdom that comes from God and His Word, we will not be able to discern truth and choose those with proven character to serve in both houses of Congress and in the White House. Keep in mind our representatives also choose the judges, cabinet members, and heads of bureaucratic agencies. Every election is important because those chosen to represent us set the course determining our future security and stability while also encouraging or encumbering the potential for success and prosperity.

While everyone may long for freedom at some level, history teaches us that people will often give up their freedom without a fight if they are promised security in return. This is a sucker's bargain!

There is, however, something even more important than elections and that is to grasp an understanding of necessary direction and corrections that must be made. If the people of a nation don't know the correct course, they will function like a mindless monstrosity. Spiritual and governmental leaders, along with all believers, must lift up a reliable standard and seek to find those who recognize its value and importance. The standard must be consistent with biblical and historically proven principles. That is not to say societies must function as a theocracy or be governed by strict scriptural interpretation but that they cannot expect to blatantly defy biblical principles and thrive.

Take divorce, for example. While the Bible prohibits divorce except for cause of infidelity, it would be difficult to enforce that standard on an entire population, especially when so many do not adhere to the authority of Scripture. But what do we see in nations where divorce is rampant and single-parent homes become the norm? Families break down. Fatherless children face all sorts of difficulties. People suffer, and consequently, so does the country.

As God becomes smaller and our all-consuming government grows larger, the value of each individual lessens. The less important the individual seems to be, the less noticed and less effectively assisted he or she will be. Meaningful assistance is the result of personal attention, interaction, and legitimate concern. When government and bureaucratic agencies become the so-called safety net, the result is insufficient care. Without what I refer to as a "compassion connection," there will be no necessary inspiration or encouragement to improve. Without personal interaction, the importance of assuming responsibility and the proper oversight requiring accountability will always be missing. Through America's many federal programs we are contributing to the people's sense of insignificance and dependence on the government rather than independence and the drive to achieve.

Without the wisdom that comes from God and His Word, we will not be able to discern truth and choose those with proven character to serve in both houses of Congress and in the White House.

Jesus did say, "To whom much was given, of him much will be required" (Luke 12:48 ESV), but He never said we are required to give it to the government. Yet we foolishly continue to tolerate this mindless practice. National leaders continually appeal to legitimate concerns to justify policies that fail and cannot be sustained.

Private sector, local community, church, and nongovernment organizations consistently prove to be more effective in assisting the poor. When government becomes involved in supporting programs that function efficiently, one of the first things they do is demand that references to God be stopped along with faith, prayer, and religious expressions. As a result, government immediately eliminates the main reason the program is successful. God, faith, prayer, love, and compassion are responsible for transforming people and nations.

People have become less interested and involved in the plight of the poor in America because assisting the poor is now almost fully under the government's control. There is growing resentment on the part of the American people because the government keeps taking more money from those who pay the taxes to support proven-to-fail policies and programs. The government keeps demanding more from the taxpayers while at the same time blaming those who pay the most taxes to help provide assistance for the poor as being the cause of poverty. There will be no success until public, private, local, and national representatives learn how to effectively work together. Government is not the answer; it is often the biggest problem.

Substituting ineffective government programs for godly living will always prove damaging to every citizen. A government will either properly serve its citizens, or it will seductively enslave its population. More often than solving our problems, America's government adds to them.

In the twentieth century, more than one hundred million people were murdered by their own governments, and that was just in communist countries. History and Scripture agree: because of sin, governments with too much power are the worst propagators of evil and destruction known to man. As long as I live, I will stand against any power presented as or perceived to be a substitute for what God alone can do through those committed to His kingdom purpose.

Government power will increase if God's power manifested through the lives of believers diminishes. "We the People" must join together in lifting up the standard pointing to the direction necessary to bring our government under control with appropriate limited power. Founder James Madison said, "In framing a government which is to be administered by men over men, the great difficulty lies in this: you must first enable the government to control the governed; and in the next place oblige it to control itself."[1]

Chapter 27

THE CHURCH OF STATE

America's overbearing, foolish, secular theocracy is using what has been called the "church of state" to cram their self-defined values down the throats of the population and place an unbearable burden on the backs of present-day and yet-to-be-born citizens. We need a miracle from above, and God offers it freely. Now is the time for Christians to become that city on a hill that cannot be hid because God's glory is revealed through the disciples of Jesus (Matthew 5:14).

Our hope is not in any political party or politician. Our hope is in the Lord, and He works through those who love Him with all their hearts and love their neighbors as themselves. These are the people who can be depended on to inspire necessary corrections.

I had the privilege of visiting with Kevin Miller, a gifted writer, businessman, and founding dean of Colorado Christian University School of Business. He shared with me his legitimate concerns for our nation. In a book titled *Freedom Nationally, Virtue Locally—or Socialism*, Kevin expounded on these concerns and the inspiration necessary to preserve and strengthen true freedom.[1] It was the first time I had heard the term *secular theocracy* and the enforcement arm referred to as *the church of state*, which is political correctness.

When Americans ask the government to deliver both freedom and virtue, they will ultimately get neither. The bigger government gets, the more people depend on it and the more insignificant and less productive they become.

For many years I have been encouraging people to pray for our "ship of state" to be turned from moral and economic danger toward safety and security. Individuals will most certainly determine their own course, but it will take wise, committed people coming together, united in purpose, to turn our nation. The supposedly indestructible *Titanic* needed to turn from hidden icebergs. It did not, and it went down. Our nation needs to turn from out-of-control, all-consuming, misdirected federal government, which has continually drifted toward becoming a secular theocracy. This power is effectively using the church of state to enforce its view of essential doctrines. Let me touch on some of our government's doctrines that Kevin Miller listed in his thought-provoking book.

The doctrine of "using deliberately mushy words and terminology." Straightforward, accountable definitions don't work to get the results desired. Terms such as *justice* won't do. Instead, the church of state uses phrases such as *social justice* because no one can really define what that means. They use the vitally important word *justice* within their phrase because this works to condemn people who aren't moved to do something—something really important, urgent, and necessary as conveniently defined by those in the secular theocracy.

The doctrine of "never enough." No matter how nonbelievers try to comply with the mushy definitions of needed secular virtues as defined by the federal government, their efforts are never enough. More taxes and federal programs are always necessary.

The doctrine of "the federal government always defines neighbor." The secular theocracy must have complete control over the definition and classifications of *neighbor*. For example, a Mexican citizen illegally in the United States taking advantage of various US taxpayers' social services—well, he's definitely a *neighbor* for secular theocracy purposes. That's because he's a voting constituent created merely by his presence on US soil. A workable and compassionate solution can be found to benefit everyone involved, but the secular theocracy would rather define those who disagree with them as racist. To a secular theocracy, a racist is whatever is defined by the government as unacceptable in order to suit its purposes of the moment, time and again. (A personal note: I see all who suffer and need help as a neighbor. I am thrilled people want to come to America to build a better life. I am, however, opposed to anyone disregarding the law.)

The doctrine of "the federal government commands how Americans will love their neighbors." Secular theocracy's social justice demands that Americans love their neighbors, but that isn't the end of the story. Citizens must love their neighbors exactly how the federal government instructs them to do so. Here's an example of how loving your neighbor works according to the federal government. Private organizations who are not secular theocracy–friendly are compelled to embrace the transgendered person ("God made me this way") while the billionaire who employs thousands of people and earns piles of money ("God made me this way") is punished by extracting taxes on the fruits of his compulsive, unappealing behavior. Of course, to the government, it doesn't matter how God really makes a person. It's up to the secular theocracy to determine what is good and what is bad, according to the political needs of the moment.

The doctrine of "results don't matter—only good intentions matter." Whether before a federal social-justice program starts or after it fails, the federal government's activities are entirely justified by its good intentions. The cost to the taxpayers is simply not important.

The doctrine of "rules about rules." The secular theocracy has rules about its rules that are to be communicated to ordinary citizens. First, the rules are made by someone other than you. Second, specific enforcement of the rules is determined at the whim of someone other than you. Third, the specifics of the rules may change at any time. Fourth, the rules may change at any time without notice.

The doctrine of "only the federal government can solve these problems." Got a business too big to fail? Got a huge social-justice opportunity? Well, friend, in a secular theocracy, the only answer is the federal government.

Now, please keep in mind that these doctrines are being forced on us by people whom our citizens put in power. Many of the people who are most greatly concerned about the problems didn't even participate in the process of selection—and if they did vote, they voted from a very uninformed position. As a result, we now have a secular theocracy with doctrines enforced by its church of state, which they are convinced is a superior belief system because they know what's best for all the rest of us. (Let me strongly emphasize that America will never have a religious or spiritual theocracy, or a state controlled by religion, because people of true faith would never tolerate it.)

It is time for people who know the truth to start demonstrating it or we might as well reinstate Pharaoh himself, submit to bondage, and get ready for the day when we will, as with Old Testament Israel, be forced to make bricks without straw (Exodus 5:18).

We need not pray for a deliverer. The Deliverer has already come and lives in every believer. It is time for us to stand up and once again embrace the freedom offered by nature's God and our nation's founders. It will take prayer, God's wisdom, and relentless determination to do God's will, beginning in our personal lives. The necessary correction will come from the bottom up, from hearts committed to God—not from top down, by foolishly trusting in mere men. If we will lift God up, then He will lift us up.

Chapter 28

WHAT, NOT WHO

The older I get, the more significant each election seems to be. When believers approach an election, we must first understand *what* must be done before we can identify *who* can best help do it. Perhaps as important now as any time since our nation's founding, those who believe in divine providence and eternal principles must become well informed and actively involved in the political process. Christians, pastors, and church leaders must totally reject the lie that "separation of church and state" means that people of faith must remain silent, uninformed, and uninvolved. Those who recognize truth and stand for it can turn the tide.

Our nation's founders knew that the limits of the Constitution were placed on the government, not on the people or religion. The right to stand up and support first principles is both a privilege and a responsibility. True freedom grants citizens the *right* to choose, and we have a *responsibility* to choose *right*. The Bible declares, "Righteousness exalts a nation" (Proverbs 14:34). The psalmist affirms, "Blessed is the nation whose God is the LORD" (Psalm 33:12). "When the righteous increase, the people rejoice" (Proverbs 29:2).

The only solid ground on which individual lives, families, communities, and nations can safely build is the foundation consistent with unshakable biblical truth. When the weight of God's kingdom impacts earth, we will clearly witness the footprints of our Father in heaven revealed through yielded lives, wise leadership, and enforceable laws and national policies. The stage is set for a spiritual awakening. Now is the time for Christians to stand together as a mighty army in the face of all evil—even when it masquerades as the source upon which people are encouraged to depend.

The correct question that demands our focused prayer and active participation is, "*What* must we do?" rather than "*Whom* should we elect?" When the citizens know the *what*, they will insist the *who* makes the right decisions or put them out of office as soon as possible. If all professing Christians, both Protestant and Catholic, along with Jewish people and those who believe the Bible is reliable, will stand together, then the foundations of our nation will be restored, the walls of protection will be rebuilt, and the people will have reason to rejoice.

Along with many national and church leaders, I am seeking to know what must be done in order to effectively deal with present-day challenges. We must hold fast to moral principles and also make wise decisions concerning fiscal policies and practices. Some legislation and policies may be well-intentioned and based on sound moral principles, but they don't work because they are based on bad economics. There is a difference between a principle and a policy.

For instance, you might believe that since God is concerned about the poor (a principle), we should raise the minimum wage to $1,000 an hour and then everyone would be rich (a policy). But believing won't make it so. The policy would create massive unemployment whether we like it or not. Permit me to share some of the obvious *whats* to consider while seeking divine guidance. It is important to recognize:

- As the Pledge of Allegiance states, we are a nation under God. And as our currency proclaims, our trust is in God—not in "gov." If national leaders do not acknowledge what America's founders understood concerning the importance of divine providence, then there will be no recovery.
- All life must be protected and seen as precious with unlimited potential, however unexpected or planned for. Remember, we can learn from Nazi Germany—specifically from their horrific extermination of the Jews and others considered less than perfect or unimportant—that something can be legal but also very evil.
- America must stand in the best interests of Israel against the evil forces calling for its destruction.
- Marriage is between a man and a woman and must be viewed as sacred. The strength of our nation depends on strong families, and national policy must protect marriage.
- There are moral absolutes. No person's failure reduces or

redefines the standards carved in stone by the finger of God and revealed in His Word. We must find a way to stop judges and courts from misinterpreting the Constitution and writing their own laws.

- Success and prosperity may be mishandled by some, but the potential for success that produces opportunity for all and prosperity at different levels is not the problem. Those we elect must keep the free market free, healthy, and under the influence of people who understand the importance of personal responsibility.

- There are forces of good and evil, and they must be wisely and rightly defined, discerned, and resisted. A strong national defense is critical. Radical Islam and terrorism are serious threats. Extreme environmental activism is as well.

- Depending on the federal government as our source is idolatry. We must control it, or it will control us. Stop the madness! Hitler believed that Germany needed a government *over* the people, not *of* the people. May God deliver us from this kind of insanity.

- Out-of-control spending, mismanagement of the people's money, and excessive, intrusive regulation is as wrong and immoral as stealing. Spending must be brought under control now, at whatever sacrifice. This does not include foolishly giving the government more of the people's money to waste or mismanage.

- "We the People" must be understood to mean that we are all responsible. We can't just lay the responsibility on others, no matter how many twisted thinkers try to play the blame game. The opportunities and possibilities to succeed are not the problem. Don't blame opportunity; instead, begin inspiring and teaching responsibility. We must find a way for every citizen to help shoulder the load in some way. This can be accomplished without being unfair or riding on anyone's back.

- Deal with excessive, foolish taxation and revamp the tax code along with the IRS so we can rejoice together as it stimulates economic growth. This would create jobs and ultimately enable us to better assist the suffering, the weak, the helpless, and the poor—not with just a handout, but with compassionate hands extended. The church can and must set the example.

- Let the people go. Turn them loose and behold the miracle made possible when people are truly free to be productive while assuming personal responsibility. Nehemiah rebuilt the wall around Jerusalem in fifty-two days (Nehemiah 6:15). Impossible? Not with God!

- The church must be delivered from the spirit of religion and filled with the Holy Spirit, leading us to the supernatural unity that produces holy harmony. National leaders must rise above partisanship and reason together, seeking effective solutions to serious challenges.

Now is the time for us to become the city set on a hill that *cannot* and *will not* be hidden. This is the time for action. God is eager to make up for the years the locusts have eaten and to reveal His love and His ways to those living in darkness, who are controlled by a worldview that denies, minimizes, or ignores God's truth. Never doubt: it is the enemy's desire to bring all of God's creation into bondage and defeat, ultimately leading to destruction. God and His truth offer fullness in life, fruitfulness, and freedom manifested by abundant life with or without the abundance of material possessions.

The sad fact is, many people—including Christians—have not handled blessings and prosperity well. The church has grown in character and strength more through persecution and poverty than in prosperity. Do not make the mistake, however, of interpreting this as the perfect will of God. It is not! God wants us to live as overcomers in this life—trusting Him, living in promised land blessing, enjoying all things richly, enduring all things, assisting those who suffer, and rejoicing continually when facing trials or when exalted beyond measure.

I am declaring to everyone with ears to hear: Now is the time to return to God. Stand up like a mighty army! Pierce the darkness, storm the gates of hell, set captives free, correct our course, reclaim the land, make God the *who* in our personal and national life, and point people to the *what*. We will never find the right *who* until we know the right *what*. When the population understands *what* to do, we can find *who* to help lead and insist that every *who* does the right *what*.

Be assured when the Lord is our Shepherd, He leads us to lie down in green pastures, not a barren desert, and beside still waters, not devastating storms (although He surely helps us overcome their impact). He comforts us in the valley of death, defeat, or despair. Even while we are facing enemies, He prepares a table before us and anoints our head with the oil of His abiding presence. May we together run to the shelter of the Shepherd who will lead us to *what* and *who*.

Every election says something about who and what the American people trust. All candidates and parties stress the importance of trust. The fact is, they each want you to trust their leadership and promises, but if you read between the lines and have the ability to discern, you will see far more. No candidate is perfect, and there are reasons for legitimate concern with most every politician. We all want both parties to be concerned with the welfare of the poor, seek better ways to enable the health-care system to work more efficiently and effectively, provide for the defense of the nation, rein in spending, and enforce constitutional laws.

Some things, however, are very clear: One party favors limited government and believes in the ability of citizens to be more productive on their own. The other believes government is the primary source of care and that financial resources should be taken from successful people and redistributed to others in order to pay for highly comprehensive social programs. I want to believe that all candidates genuinely care about others, so how to best care for others, especially those with legitimate needs, is the real question.

In Luke's gospel, we hear this account of Christ on the topic of money: "Someone in the crowd said to Him, 'Teacher, tell my brother to divide the family inheritance with me.' But He said to him, 'Man, who appointed Me a judge or arbitrator over you?' Then He said to them, 'Beware, and be on your guard against every form of greed; for not even when one has an abundance does his life consist of his possessions'" (12:13–15). Jesus continued with His theme of a greater kingdom, declaring the fact that He was more concerned with His kingdom on earth than earthly possessions. Yet liberals love to drag Jesus into their arguments for the redistribution of wealth. They are typically less concerned with Scripture than with finding an excuse for some form of socialism.

This is what Dr. Craig Vincent Mitchell calls the "gospel of big government." He goes on to explain the ramifications:

> What liberals actually offer is the gospel of big government. Big government is the kind of god that they can depend on, because it takes care of the poor by providing them with a life that is not dependent on merit, hard work, or morality. In fact, it is the kind of god that welcomes immorality of all sorts. Consequently, the god of big government does everything to make sure that people have a right to abortions, homosexuality (and other alternative sexualities) and more importantly, big government treats everyone equally (as a number). The god of big government offers safety (at the cost of freedom), but he is not a good god.[1]

The people must control the government, or the government will control the people. "We the People" will ultimately trust either God or government. If the government does not serve us wisely and effectively, then we will serve it to our own ruin.

When people are taught to look to government or to others to care for them, they will not look to God. God must be our source. The prophet Jeremiah said, "Cursed is man who trusts in mankind" (Jeremiah 17:5). When people in trouble are led or encouraged to look to politicians and the federal government for help, they will not seek God and find the real assistance they desperately need. When "We the People" are taught not to notice, love, care for, or assist our neighbor, we too have been deceived and contribute to our own downfall, loss of freedom, and ultimate bondage. Handing our personal responsibility and the importance of being involved in meeting the needs of others to some agency or national political power destroys hope.

If the American people will again put God in first place, we will notice others and, motivated by true compassion, work together to find meaningful solutions. In addition, we will be personally involved. People in need must see people who care in order to recognize there is a God who also cares. A government program will not, and should not, be expected to reveal the love of God. Trusting government to care for the poor strips God from the equation. This is not biblical compassion.

I am not opposed to a "safety net" approach to welfare, but we are now at the point of providing "ladders" to everyone who feels they need to move upward. Even worse, we are not approaching the solutions with the idea of producing more wealth but rather with the idea of viewing wealth as a fixed amount that must be reapportioned in order to benefit others. As we cave in to the desires of activists, such as taxpayer-provided condoms for graduate school students, we depart the realm of assisting the poor and enter into a true socialist society. This is not the America that surpassed the world in wealth, strength, freedom, and positive influence.

People's needs and weaknesses should help drive them to the

correct source of help: God. Instead, we are training them to turn to government. A faceless federal agency sending out checks with no personal connection is welfare, but it is not compassion in the scriptural sense. If "We the People" keep lifting up the government rather than God and His love as the answer to life's challenges, then we are actually promoting idolatry. Pointing people to government for assistance instead of stepping up and, as the church of Jesus Christ, taking an active, personal hand in helping others is a complete abdication of the call of God. May God forgive us and lead us to repentance!

Our presidential elections give us an indication of whom and what the American people trust. If we say no to ever-increasing debt, overreaching entitlements, more taxes (ultimately on everyone), then we will also be saying yes to personal responsibility, meaningful acts of compassion, legitimate interest in our neighbors, and a determination to offer assistance by mentoring others.

This is the only way out, and we must do it together as "We the People," under God, indivisible. Then, and only then, will we have liberty, justice, and hope for all. We will again be the land of opportunity and a "shining city on a hill"[2] for all the world to admire. It is not too late, but it is late. Watch and pray—and vote!

PART
EIGHT

EVERY LIFE MATTERS

When a movement sprang up in 2013 and grew to prominence the next year, the phrase "Black Lives Matter" became controversial. During the first Democratic debate of 2015, the candidates were asked, "Do black lives matter, or do all lives matter?"[1]

I understand the social and political undertones implied in that question, but it's really not an either/or situation. Black lives matter precisely because all lives matter. It's scandalous that there would ever be a debate about either question. Only in the realm of human corruption could that question even be posed.

In God's view, and therefore in the eyes of those with a godly worldview, every life matters—every color, male and female, young and old, sick and healthy, rich and poor, famous and un- known. Every single person is "fearfully and wonderfully made"

(Psalm 139:14). Failure to understand this truth and implement it in society has led to a catastrophic amount of human suffering, from slavery and oppression to abortion and genocide. If any society wants to thrive, it must sear into its national conscience these three words: *every life matters*.

Chapter 29

EQUAL VALUE AND DIGNITY

The Declaration of Independence describes as a self-evident truth, "that all men are created equal, that they are endowed by their Creator with certain unalienable Rights, that among these are Life, Liberty, and the pursuit of Happiness." Life is the first right. Without it, you can't enjoy any other right.

Everyone knows vaguely that man is more than a mere animal, but most ancient cultures had a much lower view of human life than we do. America emerged from a culture that had been taught for centuries the biblical truth that each of us, male and female, is created in the image of God (Genesis 1:27). We still have a hard time applying this truth consistently, and the culture of death seeks to erase it from our cultural memory. Yet the truth still haunts the minds of Americans, even those who insist there is no God.

Unfortunately, secularism and progressivism have eroded this belief. Progressive Charles Merriam once wrote, "Rights are considered to have their source not in nature, but in law."[1] Alas, what the government giveth, the government taketh away, as we have learned in spades since *Roe v. Wade*. A culture once committed to life now risks being consumed by the culture of death.

Against this, we must proclaim that the twelve-week-old unborn baby sucking her thumb, the handicapped infant, the elderly widower hooked up to an oxygen tank, and the people we don't think contribute to society are valuable simply by virtue of being human. They don't earn their value, and the government does not bestow it upon them. A just and humane government recognizes, in its laws, the equal value of every human being. The first duty of government is to protect the right of innocent human beings not to be destroyed by others. Pull out that thread and eventually the whole tapestry will unravel.

The right to private property, to enjoy the fruits of our labor, is closely linked to our right to life. Our property is, in a sense, an extension of ourselves; it is intimately wrapped up in our God-given role as stewards. So a right to property also protects our right to life. This is why no coherent defense of the right to property will deny the right to life.

Because Christians believe that every human being has value, we treat extreme poverty, disease, and death as enemies rather than just bad karma. We can't create heaven on earth, but we should act and support policies that lift people out of extreme poverty in the long run.

None of this is to say that we all have, or even should have, the same skills, motivation, or economic value. In announcing his

Great Society initiative, President Lyndon Johnson asserted that "we seek not just equality as a right and a theory but equality as a fact and equality as a result."[2] No. This is to seek what cannot be had—unless we merely want equality in misery. Bitter experience teaches us that trying to establish an equality of outcome among diverse individuals is not only counterproductive but it violates justice and our dignity as individuals. While insisting that we are created equal, we must also protect our diversity.

Chapter 30

THE FIRST ISSUE

I am astounded by the number of people who claim to be Christians yet directly or indirectly support abortion on demand. Even those who put their faith in science reject the simple truth revealed in a sonogram: life begins before birth. "Before I formed you in the womb I knew you, before you were born I set you apart," the prophet Jeremiah attributed to God (Jeremiah 1:5 NIV). People may dismiss that as ancient poetry, but it takes a more aggressive betrayal of the intellect to willfully ignore modern science.

As a society, we call the termination of a one-hour-old infant "murder." Yet if the pregnancy is terminated one hour prior to delivery? That's just a "woman's right." Does anyone really believe the fetus is magically transformed during that two-hour period? Sure, there is a drastic change in the mother's body as she amazingly delivers the life she has nurtured for nine months or so and ushers the newborn child into the world, but the newborn infant is remarkably the same whether inside the womb or outside. As the child gasps its first breath and shifts from umbilical cord nourishment to mother's milk, he or she does not immediately sprout limbs, grow eyes and ears, or experience its first brain activity. These things were already there, as were other human phenomena such as hiccupping, dreaming, sucking the thumb, and feeling pain. Yet society consents to taking that life, and many professing believers enable it by supporting politicians who advocate abortion and allowing their tax dollars to go to organizations that encourage and/or perform abortions.

And then comes the perplexing hypocrisy. Many of these same people of faith pay lip service to hot-button issues like "human rights" or "women's health" or "caring for the poor." They use words like *responsibility* or *compassion* or even *freedom*. But none of these things can exist when we ignore the first issue, which is the right to life.

Our Founding Fathers ordered life correctly in the Declaration of Independence: "We hold these truths to be self-evident, that all men are created equal, that they are endowed by their Creator with certain unalienable Rights, that among these are Life, Liberty and the pursuit of Happiness." The first right, given by our Creator and evident to those with eyes to see, is "Life." After that, we are able to discuss "Liberty." Once those two things are settled, we can examine "the pursuit of Happiness." Without the foundation of life, no argument on behalf of the next two issues can be safely constructed.

Whenever pro-choice proponents decide to discuss health

insurance, claiming to be compassionate toward those who are involuntarily (and even voluntarily) uninsured, their words are largely meaningless because they will not ensure the health of a life in the womb. While activists of color attempt to spotlight human rights violations, most cover up the fetal genocide going on in the African American community. When feminists cry for equal pay in the workplace, some forget that an unborn girl cries for equality in the first place. When immigration activists demand the unfettered crossing of borders, many conveniently shut down the most innocent person's passage of life.

Those who wish to discuss, promote, campaign on, raise funds with, or champion the cause of liberty or the pursuit of happiness cannot legitimately do so until they champion the cause of life. One cannot take the second or third step without taking the first.

People caught in this charade will mock those who bring it up as narrow-minded and unsophisticated. But ask anyone who has faced a life-threatening situation: "Is any issue more important than life?" I can promise you that those people scrambling to get out of the World Trade Center on 9/11 cared nothing about their work duties that day. Nobody bemoaned a missed meeting or an incomplete spreadsheet. They were not concerned about health care or equal pay. They didn't care at all about social, political, or religious matters. They cared about one thing: getting out alive. They weren't narrow-minded; they were clear-headed. They knew what was important.

Too many people have lost that ability to think clearly. Their minds are muddled with side issues, good intentions, and false promises. They have fallen for rhetoric and failed to see reality. A nation cannot continue killing its children and expect to escape the consequences. We need not tremble at the judgment of God as much as the fruit of our own savagery. God wants to save us from the effects of our hideous sin, but those who do not change their ways refuse His rescue.

I will not endorse any politician who advocates abortion. His or her party affiliation does not matter one bit. His or her abilities on second and third issues do not count if he or she has missed the first one. Any Christian who supports such politicians, even with a single vote, must ask whether this could ever be acceptable in the eyes of God. Would God really say, "I know this politician approves of children being killed the day before I was going to bring them into the world, but have you heard his speech on health care?" Not a chance. People who put more faith in science and logic must ask, "Since life clearly begins prior to birth, should we not fight for their human rights?" Obviously we should.

A nation cannot continue killing its children and expect to escape the consequences.

The series of undercover videos in 2015 that exposed Planned Parenthood should make everyone stop and think. There is no denying that a nongovernmental organization that receives taxpayer funding is actively promoting, participating in, and possibly profiting from the abortion industry. Had Planned Parenthood been active at the time of my birth, I probably would not have been born. Four generations of the Robison family—with three children, eleven grandchildren, and a first great-grandson—never would have been. Perhaps my tiny body parts would have been sold to the highest bidder.

It is unimaginable what a once-great nation is not only tolerating but defending and even supporting with our tax dollars—all without the consent of over half of the population. Thank God for the courageous, God-loving, life-loving remnant who value life so much that they are willing to stand up against the hellish assault on precious, innocent life.

Elections are not just about abortion. There are many other important issues. Many good and smart people have different views on the various challenges we face individually and as a nation. But we cannot take the second step with any politician until he or she has taken the first step by vowing to protect innocent human life.

Chapter 31

CELEBRATION OF LIFE

W hy is the Friday before Easter referred to as Good Friday, when Christ's death was visibly gruesome and awful? It is because Christ's death—the sacrifice He made for us—was an expression of the grace and goodness of God. The word *celebration* may not seem appropriate for an occasion that marks history's darkest day and humanity's brightest hope, but we certainly understand the importance of celebrating His glorious resurrection with indescribable gratitude. Every person should gladly receive the resurrection life Christ offers because we can experience the fullness of life through it. I don't think there has ever been a time of greater need for those who profess faith in Christ to experience the fellowship of His suffering and the power of His resurrection.

Paul understood the importance of Christ's suffering because it was clearly an expression of His love and compassion. Many people have become convinced that church people do not care about others. Nothing could be further from the truth for those who truly know the Lord Jesus. You see, it is the transforming power of His life and love that leads to the manifest power of true redemption. This is a far cry from mere religion. This is new life, which leads us to pursue the knowledge of God our Father—who is not merely the Father in heaven but lives in our hearts. His love fills us, spilling over like a river of life in loving expressions toward others.

We should also ask how it is that committed Christians can tolerate what has now become America's holocaust. Hitler killed eleven million people because he deceived and manipulated them into allowing the annihilation of innocent men, women, and children. He even convinced the Jews on their way to the gas chambers that he was taking them to safety and security—a better place. Since 1973, America has institutionalized the slaughter of innocent babies in the wombs of their mothers. The American people have not adequately defended the preciousness of life. Always remember: when you devalue any life, you have devalued all life. We will continue to witness the ever-increasing number of elderly and senior citizens and those who have health challenges become less important to many Americans, even to their own families.

How have these trends gained momentum? It is because the transforming resurrection power of Christ has been replaced with mere religious consent or church membership. It is obvious Christians have not been leading people to Christ. Their witness is weak or missing. Unless hearts are changed and minds renewed by the Holy Spirit, people will not think right or live right, and they certainly won't vote right. Most professing Christians don't vote. If they did and voted on biblical principles, we would not be on our present disastrous course because Christians are by far the largest identifiable percentage of the population.[1]

It's not a matter of imposing our Christian principles and beliefs on unbelievers. That will only lead to even greater rebellion, resistance, and polarization. There will never be a substitute for the transforming power of the cross of Christ, true spiritual redemption, and living the resurrected life of Christ.

No true believer would ever put down someone who is trapped by desires and appetites or hindered by weakness any more than he or she would belittle someone who has experienced the tragic consequences of a divorce. True believers, above all people on this planet, must freely manifest the love of God expressed on Good Friday when Jesus said, "Father, forgive them; for they do not know what they are doing" (Luke 23:34). In other words, they are being held captive by a power beyond themselves, which is so true of many. This is why we must be eager and free to offer grace and forgiveness.

The American people have not adequately defended the preciousness of life. Always remember: when you devalue any life, you have devalued all life.

At the same time, we do not endorse or embrace choices that are contrary to the Word of God. Many people are held captive by their desires, appetites, and addictions. Those who are defeated should diligently seek to find help and bring their actions in line with truth and true freedom, which is the liberty and overcoming grace that can be found in the Christ.

We must never change God's Word to accommodate anyone's faulty choices. We ask God to grant us the grace and ability to see our actions brought in line with His Word and truth. It is truth that makes us free, and only truth can keep us free. God's Word is truth, and the Jesus who was raised on Easter is alive to live in us with delivering power. He has sent the Holy Spirit to indwell us and to enable us to overcome temptation. Our temptation does not disappear, but Jesus offers us the power to prevail. Believers don't have to live in defeat as prisoners to unbridled passions. We can live as overcomers experiencing the liberating power of God.

When asking the very important question, "What are we to do about our nation's direction?" one might answer, "We need to elect principled leaders with strong character." This is true, but keep in mind that misguided, misdirected, and deceived people do not recognize good leaders, and many people who decide to run for office live unprincipled lives controlled by deception. How are we going to know what is best? We can perceive the best choice only by putting aside the deeds of darkness and fixing our eyes on Jesus, committed to the Word that God has given us to guide our steps.

I am convinced that every priest, pastor, preacher, politician, parent, business leader, and laborer needs a fresh encounter with Christ. As Jesus said, everyone must experience a spiritual new birth (John 3:3), and even those who have been spiritually re-born are in obvious need of a present-day spiritual awakening. Believers need to experience what the apostle Paul referenced as the "fellowship of His sufferings" (Philippians 3:10). We need to identify in a personal way with what is on our Lord's heart. First we identify with His concerns, and then we experience the power of His resurrection.

The main reason our nation gropes in darkness right now is because people who claim to know the light and who are called to be light in this world have allowed that light to be hidden, covered, and even compromised. Wouldn't it be wonderful if Christians would recommit wholeheartedly their lives to the Lord Jesus and His Great Commission (Mathew 28:19–20)—to be disciples and witnesses on this earth, here at home and around the world for His glory?

It is very important for every American to be praying for our leaders, to be concerned about our nation's direction, to care about our neighbors—and yes, to even hope for great leadership and principled election results. Every Christian must know this: winning elections is not nearly as important as winning hearts and minds. Until people's hearts are changed by the power of God and their minds are renewed by the truth of His Word, we won't have qualified leaders with the necessary character and strength for their elected offices. Without changed hearts and renewed minds, we will not have voters with the integrity, wisdom, discernment, and understanding necessary to choose those who can best lead.

Until Americans correctly choose this day whom they will serve (Joshua 24:15), they are going to be slaves to out-of-control appetites, compulsive behaviors, lack of sensitivity, diminishing compassion, bad judgment, and ever-increasing, unbearable bondage. Only Jesus can break the shackles, set the captives free, and give us the hope, peace, and security our hearts long for and everyone deserves. God the Father so desires this for us that

He gave His Son to pay the price for our sins and raised Him to live in us—to give us life now and forever (John 3:16).

A phrase we often hear from the lips of politicians and public speakers in their closing remarks is, "God bless America!" We might better ask, "When will America and our citizens once again wholeheartedly seek to bless God?"

Chapter 32

THE PRECIOUS IS TRAMPLED

In the Sermon on the Mount, Jesus told His followers they were to be "salt" and "light" (Matthew 5:13–14). The light should not be covered in any way but prominently display its illuminating power—dispelling the darkness and revealing the way. During Christ's time, salt was used to preserve that which is precious. It had a powerful effect unless it lost its savor, as Jesus said. If it did, then it was "no longer good for anything, except to be thrown out and trampled under foot by men" (v. 13).

Because the light of Christ has been dimmed by compromise, lack of compassion, and comfort-seeking compatibility with like kind rather than Christlike witnesses, we suffer prevailing darkness, deception, and destruction in America and around the world. People seem unable to find their way because they have missed or rejected "the way, and the truth, and the life" Jesus freely offers (John 14:6). Too many church folks have become just that:

church folks, rather than Spirit-filled, love-filled, bold witnesses. Because the Christian witness has not been expressed consistently with conviction and made a kingdom imprint on the culture, that which is precious is now being trampled underfoot. The burden of the Lord today is for the church He purchased to rise up and fulfill its calling. The nations are reaping the bad fruit of a garden neglected by the church.

Precious, innocent, unborn babies are mercilessly killed in the wombs of the mothers, disregarding the basic natural tendency to love and nurture the child. Why do not all believers weep over the now-accepted, promoted practice of abortion and help stop this modern-day holocaust? It is only when people are inspired to understand the preciousness of all life and its unlimited potential that they will stop the slaughter.

The sanctity of the marriage commitment and vows is of little value to most couples today, with a significant number of marriages among professing Christians ending in divorce. Relationships, at best, seem strained and weak. Couples now live together, "hooking up" rather than making covenant vows. Today same-sex partners demand their personal desires, appetites, and practices be called something they will never actually be. Their relationship will never be what God established and ordained as marriage—which can, by nature, only be between a man and a woman.

Family is now redefined by secular, progressive activists as any group or community claiming to be a family. Government no longer serves the people but openly tramples the rights granted us by nature's God and nature's law and established by our founders in the Constitution. Freedom is now defined as the right to do what anyone wants rather than the ability to live under control doing what is best as responsible citizens. Lawlessness prevails because God's law is ignored and cast aside.

When the walls of protection had been torn down and the gates of the city set on fire by the enemy, Nehemiah called the people and inspired them to stand together against the skeptics and mockers while they courageously built the walls in just fifty-two days (Nehemiah 6:15). It was a miracle of faith and working in unity with purpose that brought about the miracle.

I asked neurosurgeon Dr. Ben Carson on *LIFE Today*, "Can we correct our course and get back on stable ground and security, and see a future and bring this out-of-control government under control? Could that happen in fairly short order?"

Dr. Carson said, "I think if we reform the tax system, take the heavy foot of the government off the neck of business and industry, and bring back our Judeo-Christian values, the United States will be there in no time."

It's not too late to avoid the coming catastrophic effects of bad decisions. In other words, a wise crew could miss the iceberg, save the ship, and begin to direct everyone toward safe harbor. This is what must happen.[1]

In the book of Lamentations, Jeremiah observed the destruction of Jerusalem and asked tearfully, "Is it nothing to all you who pass this way?" (1:12). He said, "For these things I weep; my eyes run down with water; because far from me is a comforter, one who restores my soul. My children are desolate because the enemy has prevailed" (v. 16). What had happened to cause him to weep and cry out for repentance, a return to God and hope for restoration?

Jeremiah described the problem, saying that no one would have believed it, even if they had been told. "The kings of the earth did not believe, nor did any of the inhabitants of the world, that the adversary and the enemy could enter the gates of Jerusalem" (Lamentations 4:12). No one believed that the enemy (Babylon) could actually enter the city of Jerusalem and destroy the worship and witness of the people, as well as the productivity and fruitfulness of the land. No one believed that a great nation set apart and called by God to bless God and bless others could be so terribly defeated. Why did it happen? "Because of the sins of her prophets and the iniquities of her priests" (v. 13). Perhaps their greatest iniquity was neglect of God's Word and indifference toward the obvious idolatry.

The shepherds who were sent by God to inspire believers to be love- and truth-filled, bold witnesses as salt and light had failed in the Old Testament, just as they have failed today. The Old Covenant people missed God, and the New Covenant people broke their relationship through disobedience and indifference. Great responsibility for the precious being openly trampled underfoot rests on the shoulders of our spiritual shepherds and people who profess to know Christ but do not bear eternal fruit.

Too many believers discuss Scripture, debate it, dissect it, and defend it—but they do not demonstrate its power by doing what it says. At best, they have heard the word but they have not done the word. They are "hearers" and not "doers" (James 1:22). Some never really hear the word—they just hear non-transforming religious messages. Believers today argue about gifts of the Spirit but don't demonstrate them. Christians fruitlessly discuss and fight over tongues, but they don't use the tongue God gave them to declare the transforming truth of the gospel in love. This must change, or the enemy will come in like a flood.

As someone wisely observed concerning the catastrophic consequences of Hurricane Katrina, New Orleans was not destroyed because of the storm; it was destroyed because the dikes failed. Today the Word of God and the witness of the church, and the kingdom power of God, represent the walls—the dikes—that God put in place to protect the people from the catastrophic effects of evil flooding the land. In many places around the world, those who profess Christ are being killed for their faith; some are being tortured and beaten before being shot. The enemy plans this for America, all Christians, and those who love freedom. The Word of God must become our hedge of protection and the walls of security as we build on the one foundation that cannot be shaken—God's Word—and the principles found there.

Now is the time for us to stand together, restore the foundation of faith and truth, and rebuild the walls of protection.

Now is the time for us to stand together, restore the foundation of faith and truth, and rebuild the walls of protection. Believers must learn to stand together in the supernatural unity Jesus prayed for in John 17. Together, we can and will witness a miracle. Don't look for an escape. Become the "shining city on a hill" with the undeniable, positive effect of salt and light.[2] Jesus is coming for an overcoming church adorned in His glory—not pressed-down, defeated, deceived, divided, or defeated. We are to overcome in this life so we can be faithful, fearless witnesses until the end.

PART

NINE

FAMILIES ARE THE FOUNDATION OF SOCIETY

God's chosen picture for the relationship between his people and Himself is that of bride and groom. His chosen analogy for the church is the family. Those institutions are His design, which is why they are under such virulent attack in our society. As Christ followers, we must not be unaware of the enemy's intent or unconcerned about the effects of this battle.

My good friend pastor Jim Garlow talks about the recurrent phrase we hear on issues related to social ills, most recently related to the attacks on marriage and family. It's the idea that "that ship has sailed." In other words, it's too late to make any change. This is an easy excuse for people who don't want to take a scriptural stance on cultural issues. But, as Garlow notes, the ships that have sailed are all doomed to sink. Like the *Titanic*,

God's people have been warning of icebergs, but those intent on sailing into destruction simply declare their ideas unsinkable and charge full steam ahead.

Garlow points to several examples in our nation's past and present where the courts and the culture sailed in the wrong direction. Slavery and civil rights are the most obvious issues where the "ship had sailed" and only an uprising against them could turn the tide. Now abortion, the rise of the welfare state, and the dismantling of marriage seem to have left the harbor with no turning back. But, Garlow says, "Real leaders don't capitulate and accommodate to the culture. They change it."[1]

The Supreme Court is not supreme. These men and women in black robes may interpret man's laws, but they cannot change God's laws. Their authority is subject to nature's law and nature's God, as our founders put it. Believers, therefore, "must obey God rather than men" (Acts 5:29) when man's laws contradict God's.

Real leaders must rise up and point our nation toward true righteousness, never giving up. We must lead by example, allowing God to restore our families in love, unity, peace, and joy in a way that even the world will envy.

Chapter 33

A FATHERLESS NATION

A huge percentage of Americans are fatherless. This reality is continually revealed by the actions and choices made by those damaged by this absence. God created us in His image to be His children. He is our heavenly Father and desires to be the most ever-present reality in every life. Adam and Eve lived in His presence. In the garden, they enjoyed intimate fellowship with their Father, experiencing the joy of His manifest presence. They were at peace, secure, living with confidence under His watch care.

Then the deceiver, the serpent, enticed them and they bought the lie, took the bait, fell, and forfeited their relationship with the Father. Adam and Eve, who knew no fear, were suddenly afraid of their own Father. They felt ashamed, naked, unclean, unworthy, and unloved, and they foolishly tried to cover their sin and shame with mere fig leaves. This was the first futile attempt on the part of fallen man to inadequately cover their shame and deal with the sinful, adverse effect of allowing themselves to be deceived by the father of all lies (John 8:44).

God the Father immediately set in motion the plan to restore fallen man to intimate fellowship with Himself. He set out to establish a family of faith through whom He would bless the nations of the world. These truly blessed and chosen children of God could reveal clearly the heavenly Father to fallen humanity.

From the time of the Fall and the sacrificial gift of Jesus Christ the Father gave to reconcile us to Himself, mankind has continually been deceived by the enemy to live as orphans without knowing a personal relationship with the one and only perfect Father. Our failure to know the Father has led to fatherless families and nations. America's fathers are too often missing, dysfunctional, idolatrous, consumed by material pursuits, or at best living with an orphan mentality.

Just as Israel did, America and the nations of the world are seeking the wrong solution to a serious dilemma. Fatherless people keep asking for a king because, as with Israel, everyone is doing "what [is] right in his own eyes" (Judges 17:6). People seek the wrong answers by establishing the wrong king and in so doing miss the necessary relationship with the Father.

We all need the King (Jesus) who will show us the Father. There is to be but one King, and this King declared, "I am the way, and the truth, and the life; no one comes to the Father but through Me" (John 14:6). No religion, no ritual, no traditions, and no idols of men can substitute for this King, who gives us the way to the Father.

We witness today in our own nation millions of citizens

seeking to find the missing father by: (1) seeking the approval of others when only God's approval will suffice; (2) engaging in compulsive behavior and addictive practices that prove to be tragic substitutes; (3) becoming pleasure seekers but remaining empty; and (4) joining something to find a sense of family or belonging (a team, club, lodge, gang, or even a religious group or church). Any family without a father—*the* Father—still reveals total emptiness.

In order to know the Father and no longer live as orphans, we must discover the one and only King and then submit our will to His. We must lose our life in His purpose in order to find it, and find it we will in all of its abundance. We must say firmly, "Your kingdom come, and our kingdom and kingdoms go!" We must understand the absolute importance of the Sermon on the Mount with special focus on Matthew 6:33 where Jesus exhorted us to seek first the kingdom of God above all else and live righteously, and He will provide everything we need. In the same chapter He referenced the evident manifestation of the Father's watch care when He said, "Look at the birds of the air . . . your heavenly Father feeds them" (v. 26). And He pointed to the fact we are of far greater value. He said, "Observe how the lilies of the field grow . . . not even Solomon in all his glory clothed himself like one of these" (vv. 28–29). If God cares for the birds and the flowers, how much more will He care for those who choose to be His children rather than live as orphans?

Many churches today are filled with people who have an orphan mentality. Jesus pointed to the cure when He told us that He has revealed the Father: "He who has seen Me has seen the Father" (John 14:9). Christ revealed the heart, character, and nature of the Father in heaven, who is to be our personal God and Father. Jesus revealed the Father's unconditional love and the power of His forgiveness—our sins gone, removed as far as the east is from the west (Psalm 103:12).

Jesus, the Lamb of God, takes away the sin of the world (John 1:29). Jesus commands us to focus on the Father and His kingdom. He must be first. The Father in heaven loves us so much that He gave His own Son to redeem us, not with silver or gold, but with the precious blood of this Lamb. His focus is on us! We focus our attention on Him and discover that He has focused His attention on us. We don't live as though it's all about us; our lives must be about Him, His kingdom, and His will being done in us on earth right now for His glory. But at the same time, the Father is vitally interested in our well-being.

People in America and around the world must recognize that there is only one way to fill the gaping hole in the human heart that is created by fatherlessness, and that is with the presence of the living God. America and the nations of the world have substituted idols for God and they have missed the Father. Our own nation, along with the nations of the world, has made a god of government while foolishly and futilely trusting the deceptive promises of mere men rather than mighty God.

I personally understand the negative effect of fatherlessness. Born the product of a forced sexual relationship to a single woman and living without a father did unspeakable damage to me as a boy and a human being. All my efforts to fill that vacuum with any source other than a relationship with God were in vain. When I gave my life to Jesus, He redeemed me and I moved from an orphan mentality to become a child of the Father. There is no substitute for this relationship. The best of earthly fathers diligently seeking to be all they should be can never fully fill the void created by man's fall from grace.

The most important contribution parents can make is to point their children to Father God. Great parents point their children to the Father. I know I missed the mark in many ways as a father, but by the grace of God our three children looked beyond this father and saw the Father and fell in love with Him. As a result, they have been effective parents and have clearly pointed to the importance of the Father, and our grandchildren have also fallen in love with Him while continually expressing their appreciation for their parents.

There are a few experiences with my father I think might be important to share. During my late teens, Joe Bailey Robison (my earthly father) spent several years in prison for various crimes. When Betty and I knew we were going to marry, my birth mother would not sign consent papers. At the time of our marriage in 1963 parental consent was required for anyone under twenty-one years of age. My father signed the consent papers while in prison. There was no doubt Betty and I were to marry, even at age nineteen. I've often said, "Thank God my father finally did something meaningful for me by enabling me to marry the beautiful, precious person I have spent my life with."

There is only one way to fill the gaping hole in the human heart that is created by fatherlessness, and that is with the presence of the living God.

After Betty and I had been married a few years and had a little girl, Rhonda, my alcoholic father suddenly entered our lives. He moved to the Houston area, and I tried to get him help with a ministry working with addicts. He did not make positive progress. One day as I drove home from San Jacinto Junior College where I was enrolled, I saw a man lying facedown in the gutter. I pulled over to see if I could help, and as I knelt down and rolled the man over, I realized it was my own father. He was in such a drunken stupor that he had fallen facedown by the curb. With the help of another passerby I was able to get him into my car, and then I took him to the mobile home that Betty and I were living in.

A few days later I put him in a room and provided the money for food and asked for someone to look after him while I took care of my family and attended classes. One afternoon when I dropped by to see him, I found that he had coerced some of the people near the complex to buy him some alcohol. He had gotten so drunk he couldn't get out of bed, and he had thrown up all over his shirt. I remember as though it were yesterday dropping down on my knees by the bed and pulling out of bed my alcoholic father, a man I had never known, who had never told me he loved me, and who never bought me a bite of food, a pair of shoes, or provided anything on my behalf. I pulled his chest up against mine and looked in his eyes and bearded face and said, "I don't know you, but I love you and I really want the best for you."

I told him about Jesus and how much God loved him. Over the coming months and years, I never saw a change in my father. I shared the gospel with him a few days before he put his head on the pillow, fell asleep, and died. He had sclerosis of the liver and diabetes from extreme alcoholism.

I hope that someday when I get to heaven and see the throngs around Jesus, there will be a hand waving through the crowd and a voice shouting, "Son, look here! It's your dad!" and discover that somehow in the last days or hours after I had witnessed to him, he invited Jesus into his heart and came to know God the Father. I believe that's possible because we have a God so full of amazing grace. That would be one of the joyful surprises in heaven if my father was there.

I wish there had been a dad in my life, but I am so grateful to know the Father anyone can know. He is indescribably awesome, full of love and mercy. He offers forgiveness and life to every person on earth. This grace gift is available to you and everyone you know.

Please hear my heart as I diligently seek to point all people to the only One who can connect you and others to the Father all hearts long for. Fatherlessness must no longer be used as an excuse for detrimental choices. I know personally that the only perfect solution to the painful scars of fatherlessness is found in the perfect Son and the perfect Father and the indwelling Spirit of both. The most important contribution we can make as parents and as Christian witnesses is to inspire people to know personally and intimately the Father in heaven by receiving the Son and yielding to His Spirit in every area of their lives.

When we put King Jesus in charge, we will begin experiencing and expressing His kingdom life. The power of this kingdom release will positively impact all earthly kingdoms and all people.

This unshakable kingdom will point people and nations to the only sound, secure, and stable foundation upon which futures can be built with meaning and purpose. Our lives will become the well-watered garden of God and an ever-flowing spring of His love. To Him be the glory forever and ever!

Chapter 34

UNNATURAL DISASTERS

In Texas, where I live, spring storms make annual appearances. Turbulent thunderstorms and tornadoes threaten people across the central plains and southeast. Betty and I pray for property and people to be spared destruction and death. In one of His greatest parables (Matthew 7:24–27), Jesus directed us all to build our house on a solid rock because the storms are sure to come, and indeed they do.

My home state set an all-time record for rainfall in 2015. Floodwaters created devastation and forced dangerous rescues. It was sad to see families lose their homes, belongings, and sometimes friends and family members. However, that crisis revealed the greatness of the love, concern, and sacrificial help of first responders. The rapid response in Texas was so effective that the media discouraged others from coming to the devastated areas. Any additional would-be volunteers were encouraged to stay home and pray.

We are grateful for our first responders. Yet having experts take care of our natural-disaster problems while volunteers sit at home isn't ideal. I don't want to see America's volunteer spirit atrophy. Sometimes, of course, we must rely on experts to safely deal with downed power lines and the like; that's understandable. But it's far from understandable, and far from acceptable, to leave the response up to the experts when the disaster is a cultural one—such as broken communities and families, out-of-control government spending, and a frontal assault on the institution of marriage.

After a natural disaster, many of us are ready and eager to join in and help—but in the midst of this unnatural disaster all across our nation, many concerned Americans are just sitting around watching it happen, hoping the experts will fix it. That makes no sense. At least with a natural disaster, we can be pretty sure that America's public servants will offer speedy help that really helps—such as clearing roads, rescuing stranded flood victims, and restoring downed power lines. But with the unnatural disaster unfolding around us, public servants all too often are making matters worse.

How so? Regarding the marriage issue, politicians and judges are attempting to redefine a bedrock cultural institution by legalizing so-called gay marriage. They might as well pass a law calling an elephant an eagle, because as soon as that elephant launches itself from a cliff, it will quickly discover that man's law doesn't nullify God's law. Those jumping on this pop culture and political bandwagon will, sadly, contribute to the downfall of many of their own family and friends.

Our public servants are making matters worse in other ways as well. For instance, in another unnatural disaster, an already difficult circumstance is often made far worse in the name of help and falsely promised hope. I am referring to political leaders and elected representatives who cause misery to individuals, families, businesses, communities, and freedom itself through their Great Society policies and agencies. They use legitimate problems to lead people into dependence and bondage. They promise to do what only God can do and what only caring, loving neighbors can accomplish. But here is the awful reality: indifferent and deceived people allow it to happen, and they don't come out to change and correct the damage. Instead, they just stumble along in prevailing darkness and deceit.

The unnatural, man-created storms I allude to are undeniable: uncontrolled, unbalanced budgets; excessive spending for unsustainable programs that have undermined fathers, families, and communities over the past half a century; and exorbitant, misdirected taxation that saps wealth-creating enterprise and teaches citizens to depend on someone or something else rather than God and their God-given creative capacity, with more and more refusing to work and become productive contributors.

Yes, some are desperate and helpless, but assistance to these needy ones must be provided by local charities that can discern their real needs and offer face-to-face compassion. A bureaucratic agency managed from afar is poorly suited for such work.

There are right ways for the government and citizens to work together, as we witness after major natural disasters. The same thing must happen now as "We the People" come out in force to stop this unnatural damage to our cities, and particularly to those communities struggling against poverty and pervasive family breakdown. The federal government has no business trying to monitor or manage people's private lives, businesses, or practices, unless someone is deliberately breaking laws necessary for civil peace and justice. Maintain that more modest mission and the government will have far more time to focus on its core roles of catching and punishing serious criminals and promoting justice and tranquility—while doing it all on a budget that won't drive our nation into bankruptcy.

It's true that private citizens too often live irresponsible, out-of-control lives that force the law to step in to protect others and serve justice. But even here the handcuffs and prison bars only get us so far. The Christian witness is what will move people and communities from brokenness to real flourishing. We must see transformed hearts, minds, and lives. My prayer and challenge is for concerned Americans to come together to stop the unnatural disaster of foolish, mismanaged, and overreaching government actions. Let's get the responsibility back in the hands of the family members, churches, and private organizations *in* the communities—freeing us to function as those who love God and our neighbors.

Chapter 35

PANDORA'S BOX UNHINGED

For years I have been seeking to help bring the family of faith together to stand against the forces of darkness, deception, and destruction. If church leaders and all who profess faith in the Lord Jesus and God as Father do not stand on behalf of marriage, the preciousness of life, and the value of freedom, as well as the personal responsibility essential to protect and preserve it, then we will lose what the grace of God, truth, love, and great sacrifice have given us the privilege to enjoy.

God established the institution of marriage before the church, before civil societies, and before government. From this God-initiated relationship of marriage, all life is formed, birthed, and given priceless oversight. We do not replace what God supernaturally created and established with anything proposed by any person, people, government, or court. Family is the first vital cell of society. It is the foundation of government. Government did not create marriage. God did.

In 2015, the US Supreme Court redefined marriage,[1] paving the way for a flood of detrimental policies and practices. Families are being destabilized, children are being raised in psychologically damaging environments, and religious freedom is being threatened. This is very serious.

It is time for the church to draw a line in the sand, a line beyond which we will not go. Whatever our denominational perspective, we must unite in our common faith in Jesus Christ. As a nation, we have lost our moral compass and face losing true freedom.

There must be a moral basis to any free society. Relativism and secularism fail to provide such a foundation. This relative view of marriage and family has led to the breakup of the family. Secularism has moved beyond simply rejecting God to declaring outright war on godly values, despite independent evidence that such values enable a more stable society.

Marriage is inherently a union between one man and one woman, beneficial to children, and the first building block of social order. Though affirmed, fulfilled, and elevated by biblical teaching, the idea of one man and one woman is not based on religion but on nature itself, ingrained in the heart and soul of humans and proven out through the exercise of reason. It enables us to govern ourselves, which is why lawlessness and anarchy become more prevalent as marriage and family deteriorate.

Government did not create marriage. God did.

Since marriage only truly works between a man and a woman, no one has any more right to gay marriage than he or she has the right to sprout wings and fly. Think of how rights work. Our government doesn't grant rights to us; it merely recognizes our existing rights. These rights were previously endowed to us *by our Creator. The government can't create rights; it can only line up with those rights given by God.*

Consider this fact: marriage existed before our ideals of individual rights or equality. In other words, marriage is a more legitimate idea than our current political system. More cultures recognize marriage than they do "gay rights," and history has validated the marital institution far more than it has democracy or a court's opinion of equality. In the pursuit of a new normal, we have undermined the very idea that there is a normal. We have cut off our legs in an attempt to jump higher.

The cry for marriage equality was always a sham because a gay man already had the exact same rights as every other man: he was free to marry one woman at a time. The honest term would be marriage "choice," meaning one can define marriage any way he or she chooses. Now that this is legal, every other marriage "choice" must be legalized to avoid discrimination. There is no rational basis for barring polygamy, group marriage, incest, and any other creation of man. The arguments used to promote same-sex unions work just as well for any voluntary arrangement imaginable. This isn't some fanciful fear tactic; it's the emerging reality. Cases are already in the courts. More will follow. Pandora's box is officially wide open.

A good government should defend marriage, but our nation's leaders have chosen to undermine it. Ultimately, the Supreme

Court has no authority to redefine marriage. Yet these unelected judges have initiated a war against our security, stability, and future. We must not idly stand by while the destruction of the sacred institution of marriage unfolds.

Experience and history have demonstrated that a legal action such as the Supreme Court has taken demands government enforcement. An escalation of police power is inevitable. Religious freedom and the right of conscience stand in the crosshairs. What was once prohibited was first tolerated and then normalized. Now that marriage choice has been declared a basic human right, it becomes a matter of justice and equality, requiring defense. It is likely that nobody will be able to publicly defend real marriage for long because longstanding, traditional views must now be deemed unlawful bigotry. Parents who object to their kindergarteners being forced to read *Keesha and Her Two Moms Go Swimming* (a real book designated as "Pre-K–2" by LGBT advocates[2]) will be treated like criminals. Churches and ministries may be forced to revise their core principles or shut down. Catholic Charities already had to abandon adoption services in California, Massachusetts, and the District of Columbia. If a religious television program preached the idea that African Americans shouldn't be allowed to marry, then we would expect them to be kicked off the air. Now that being gay has been legally equated to being black, what do we expect to happen to Christian television? Even quoting the Bible concerning homosexuality could soon be illegal.

I actually experienced this decades ago. In early 1979, our weekly television program was airing nationally on network and independent stations. On one episode, I said that homosexuality was outside of God's plan for us. I also speculated that it could be a health risk—and this was before the AIDS epidemic. In response to pressure from a gay activist, our flagship station in Dallas took our program off the air. The next week a gay-advocacy group was given the entire thirty-minute time slot.

We didn't go quietly. The public rose up in support as more than eleven thousand people gathered at a Freedom Rally to defend the freedom of speech and the right to preach. Major advertisers protested the action of the station and its national corporate owner. The station's decision eventually became national news, making its way into *People* magazine and talk shows hosted by Tom Snyder, Jerry Rose, and Phil Donahue. The backlash contributed to the demise of the misnamed Fairness Doctrine. We won the battle in 1979, but the balance of the war has drastically shifted since then.

Right now I don't see how we are not headed toward the imprisonment of pastors and other Christian leaders. I don't see how Christian media can survive. I don't see how religious schools and universities can operate without fully embracing homosexuality. I don't see how companies that don't advocate gay marriage can be allowed to engage in business.

Given all of this, I don't see how we are not headed toward civil unrest or complete collapse. That's why we need to pray—and pray hard—and come together as believers to address these critical issues. That's also why we must elect leaders who will preserve the freedom of religion enshrined in our Bill of Rights. We cannot allow the destruction of our nation to occur on our watch. This is where Christians must draw the line.

Chapter 36

NOT AN IDLE WORD

Consider the words that God wrote with His finger as the Ten Commandments on tablets of stone. The First Commandment, and the one all others ultimately depend upon, is, "You shall have no other gods before Me" (Exodus 20:3). Please take very seriously the words found in Deuteronomy 32:46–47: "Take to your heart all the words with which I am warning you today, which you shall command your sons to observe carefully, even all the words of this law. For it is not an idle word for you; indeed it is your life. And by this word you will prolong your days in the land, which you are about to cross the Jordan to possess."

Just like the Old Testament Israelites, Americans have experienced promised land blessings. Our national anthem declares we are to be known as "the land of the free and the home of the brave." Prolonging our days with the blessings only freedom makes possible depends on the response of God's church to the demands being made today by those who reject the truth as revealed by nature's God and nature's law. And this is just the beginning—but hopefully not the beginning of the end.

The church of Jesus Christ will either take a stand on God's irrefutable truth or we will witness the fall of our once-great nation. The enemy of truth and father of lies has drawn his line in the sand and demands America choose whom we will serve. Will we refuse to listen to the promises of another Pharaoh to care for us as his slaves, or will we take an even more foolish step by accepting another controlling force like Nebuchadnezzar? Remember, Nebuchadnezzar not only required servanthood, but he demanded that everyone bow down to worship his image or face the fiery furnace (Daniel 3).

Such are the threats against the church—ministers, pastors, priests, and any who refuse to compromise God's call to put a trumpet to their lips, proclaiming truth and true liberty throughout the land. The church and church leaders now face the choice either to bow before the demands and gods of this world, or, as the three Hebrew young men did, refuse to bend, bow, or break regardless of any threats. The three faithful Hebrews experienced firsthand the supernatural power of the fourth man in the midst of the fire and did not even smell of smoke (Daniel 3:27). They were, in fact, a sweet-smelling aroma to a holy and loving God. Count me in with them.

We must not stand by and accept the demands of Bible-denying, truth-denying, unprincipled people, however great their numbers, who try to force us to approve of idols and vote them into high places throughout the land, the churches, or into law.

The issue of same-sex marriage is far bigger than giving people special rights and protection that the law already guarantees and that God's people would certainly support. No one should be mistreated, even if we believe they make poor choices and participate in what Scripture deems unwholesome. But by demanding that we give same-sex couples the "right" of marriage, we are being asked to "exchange the truth of God for a lie" rather than flee idolatry (Romans 1:25), and we are being manipulated to embrace and exalt idolatry into national law. The American people are being asked to vote for idolatry, accept it, embrace it, and approve it. We are expected to call what is clearly unnatural "natural" and encourage people to live as prisoners to their own appetites whatever they may be: smoking pot, abusing drugs, engaging in extreme sexual practices—ultimately *anything goes.*

Believers are faced with a choice. Pastors, church members, and those they influence must choose whom they will bow before and serve. The choice is clear, however muddled some may try to make it. The issue is much bigger than the enemy of truth wants you to believe. Idolatry will always challenge each citizen on our own personal journey. But are we as a nation going to vote idolatry on the throne? Whatever people, parties, and practices in our day demand, will we approve it either by our consent or by our silence? Or will those who profess

The church of Jesus Christ will either take a stand on God's irrefutable truth or we will witness the fall of our once-great nation.

faith in Christ stand with as much commitment and unity as those who oppose irrefutable, undeniable, biblical truth?

Never has the call of Christ and His prayer for unity among believers been more urgently important. We must be one with the Father and perfected in unity with one another in order to take a stand against this tsunami of immorality. It's not just religious freedom that hangs in the balance. We face the extinction of the very idea of liberty.

PART
TEN

CHURCHES MUST BE AGENTS OF UNITY

Imagine how great our witness would be if only Christians would recognize that we are a family—and we can be a healthy, happy, blessed family. Every person needs and longs to be part of a family filled with love and enjoying meaningful relationships.

People join clubs, associations, lodges, churches, and other organizations, seeking to be part of a family. Teenagers who are longing for a sense of family often join gangs in an attempt to satisfy that felt need. Even members of the Mafia refer to themselves as a "family" and recognize "godfathers." The reality is, we all need Father God to discover the only way to live in joyful harmony while building our lives and relationships on sound principles that provide a sense of security and belonging. As a family the church can stand together against all assaults.

The enemy of the family is deception and dissension, leading to division and the loss of commitment, unity, and purpose. We see it in the quarreling and division in the family of believers, the church. We recognize it, but that doesn't mean we have to throw up our hands and accept it. We should all pray for the healing of our church family, referred to in the New Testament as the body of Christ, and also pray for the healing of our nation. This is the best hope for the preservation of the American dream.

Protestants, Catholics, and Orthodox Christians, let's meet at the feet of Jesus. I count among my friends Baptists, Pentecostals, Presbyterians, Methodists, Lutherans, charismatics, Catholics—I could go on and on. We disagree on things—some trivial, some not so trivial. But we all love the Lord and are seeking to follow Him. Whatever Christ-centered group you may support, let's become a family and seek the absolute best for every member.

Chapter 37

DIVINE DIVERSITY

The apostle Paul urged believers in Rome to "live in harmony with one another" (Romans 12:16 NIV). The interesting thing about harmony is that it isn't sameness. In music, one person will sing the melody. Those who sing harmony sing something that is different but fits with the melody. A good harmony singer makes the melody all that more sweet.

There is great diversity in God's church: differences in style, ceremony, emphasis, ability, and other beautiful manifestations of the vastness of our Lord. God didn't make two fingerprints, two snowflakes, or any two people the same; but with all of our diversity, we can have supernatural unity. This same supernatural power settled on the founders of the United States, enabling them to establish a foundation for our nation greater than any of the character strengths and traits they possessed individually. They were part of a miracle! We need another such miracle today. I am witnessing encouraging signs and long to be a part of the answer to Jesus's prayer in John 17—one with the Father and perfected in supernatural unity with one another.

As we respond to the ministry of the Spirit through gifted, called-out communicators of truth, we will begin to connect to one another as members of the body of Christ. As an illustration, the upper arm connects to the lower arm so that the hand functions effectively, especially if it is submitted to the head. This is a picture of the body of Christ as the members connect one to another. We can extend the hands and arms of God to a world in desperate need of the comfort that can be offered through His body when it is built up into the fullness of the stature of Christ (Ephesians 4:13).

To make it clear, when the church—the community of faith with all of its diversity and unique parts—becomes connected to one another and submitted to the Head, we will accomplish the will of God on earth. We will be the answer to His prayer, "Your kingdom come. Your will be done, on earth" (Matthew 6:10). Right here, right now, through the family of faith!

All too often, people in the church have misinterpreted making disciples to mean making members of our own group. By seeking to spiritually clone ourselves, we have succeeded in making "like kind," but we have not necessarily made "Christlike kind." If we show people that we love them—period—the way a dedicated parent loves a child, their lives can be transformed by the power of the Holy Spirit.

If you had asked me years ago if I loved other people, I would have said yes, but I had a critical spirit that was not healthy. The fact is, we hold our religious convictions even more strongly than any political concern. We often defend our beliefs in such a way that we actually contribute to our own defeat. Mean-spirited religious sectarianism has as much potential to damage people as racism or any other "-ism." God got my attention and showed me I had developed a very unloving attitude through my association with other like-minded individuals and groups.

I remember calling Billy Graham and criticizing him quite forcefully for his association with people I deemed too liberal or non-evangelical because of his friendship with Catholics in America and in other countries. I even foolishly questioned his association with charismatics and Pentecostals. Dr. Graham was unfailingly gracious to me in that conversation, and he said, "I really want to be careful that I'm not compromising. I don't want to do that. But tell me this: Do you know these people? Have you been around these people that you are talking about? Have you spent much time with them?"

I said, "No, I haven't."

He replied, "Well, I have, and I've found them to be very Christlike. As a matter of fact, I couldn't have a crusade outside the United States without their help. If it were not for the Pentecostals and charismatics, I couldn't have an effective crusade overseas."

As I look back on that conversation, I realize that the same small-mindedness and hard-heartedness I exhibited is a tendency of many in the church. And we need to stop it. It's not healthy, and it makes us insensitive to the heart of God. It deafens us to what the Lord is saying to His people. Billy Graham inspired me to spend time with Christians and church leaders I had been critical of, and I experienced the transforming power of God's love. As I got to know *them* better, I came to know *Him* better. I saw clearly there is only one perfect Person, and His name is Jesus. It is sad to realize that while attempting not to compromise, we often find ourselves compromising the Great Commandment to love God and others appropriately.

Showing love to others in the body of Christ does not mean we will never have disagreements, but let's learn how to resolve those disagreements without being hateful. What have we accomplished if we "win" a debate but lose a brother? I have been blessed beyond measure when joining with other church leaders—Protestant and Catholic and all those who confess Jesus as Lord and the Bible as His Word—to find common ground necessary to effectively address our common concerns.

When I am asked why I work with Catholics and those of different denominations, I answer, "Because I love everyone and will faithfully and without compromising faithfully seek to present God's truth in love to everyone with ears to hear. If I appear unwilling to communicate with others or hear them, how can I expect others to willingly hear me?" The fact is, we all need to be seeking to more clearly hear God. I join with Jesus in praying for the supernatural unity we have only glimpsed in history and with every visitation a spiritual awakening resulted.

Keep in mind that supernatural spiritual unity is not sameness. It is love lifting us above our differences along with necessary diversity in order to pursue common goals for the glory of God and benefit of others. It never demands that we cast aside our convictions or the truth. It is reaching out in love so we all continue to "grow in the grace and knowledge of our Lord and Savior Jesus Christ" (2 Peter 3:18). Those who believe there is a Creator and Father God who expresses His love through Christ must recognize the importance of standing together as salt to preserve the innocent and as light exposing evil and illuminating the best way in which to walk and live.

The enemies of God, faith, the Bible, moral principles, marriage, family, and the right to life will never willingly give up an inch of the ground they seek to claim and control. They are determined to manipulate, dominate, and control. They are the most intolerable people on this planet. Unless those who profess a belief in God, His Son, the Holy Spirit, and His Word as reliable begin standing together, then deception, darkness, and defeat of true freedom will result. Believers must find common ground to resist the assault on truth—or the precious, including freedom, will, as Jesus said, be "trampled under foot by men" (Matthew 5:13).

Protestants and Catholics must find ways to stand against the gates of hell while lifting up Jesus as "the way, and the truth, and the life" (John 14:6). We must make it clear that no one comes to the Father but by Him. I will never cease proclaiming this truth for all to hear. If we lose the freedom we have been blessed to enjoy in America, then voices will be silenced and open expressions of faith ended. We must protect life and freedom while exalting Christ and truth, and we must do it in love. I am committed to this until the end and will encourage those who care and love freedom to join with us.

I still have deep theological convictions, but my convictions are now aimed more toward tearing down the walls that separate people and building a dialogue that leads to healing and reconciliation. I'm tired of the division in the church and in our nation. I want to help bring people together, "speaking the truth in love" (Ephesians 4:15). Of course truth does have a polarizing effect, but when truth is shared in the power of God's love, it penetrates and influences all parties and groups for the better.

That's why I am heartbroken when church leaders and political leaders refuse to dialogue and interact honestly, refusing to hear one another. And it disturbs me when I see the media misrepresent the truth, or when I see Hollywood filmmakers misrepresent the truth, or when religious people misrepresent the truth. Let's stop hiding behind our party lines, our denominational differences, our stereotypes, and our rhetoric. Let's speak the truth lovingly to each other and continue to build on the absolute principles that have made our nation great and that must be restored.

Let's speak the truth lovingly to each other and continue to build on the absolute principles that have made our nation great and that must be restored.

There is no doubt we are facing challenges. These are perilous times and difficulties lie in wait at every turn. But if we will commit ourselves to the principle that love conquers all, then we will find God's love expressed through us is sufficient to correct our political problems and effectively meet the pressing needs people face.

Chapter 38

COMMON CONCERNS OF THE CHURCH AND STATE

O ur nation is heading in the wrong direction, and much of the responsibility lies in the church. Still, there is hope—and it lies in the church as well. Our founders understood the importance of personal freedom. Their journey toward freedom was similar to Israel's supernatural deliverance from bondage in Egypt. As surely as God sent Moses to lead the Israelites out of bondage toward the promised land, with the supernatural parting of the Red Sea and miraculous sustenance in the wilderness, our nation's founders understood they too were on a pilgrimage that required divine intervention and care of the Creator and God of Abraham, Isaac, and Jacob.

Our founders had witnessed the bondage forced on believers by ruling powers and dictatorial monarchies. They had lived through horrible abuses by the ruling classes. America offered a place to escape this oppression and to establish a nation where freedom could be protected and offered to others. There is little doubt that Moses and the Old Testament books of the law greatly impacted the thinking of our nation's Founding Fathers.

The early believers, including those on the *Mayflower* and the ministers proclaiming the gospel in the original colonies, all understood that if Christ came to set people free, then this God-given right must be pursued, established, and protected. Our founders truly understood the meaning of freedom. They understood that the individual must remain free, not the subject of any earthly ruling power, in order to fully receive the benefits and prosperity freedom offers. This is why they so emphatically established what was to be a limited government. They made it clear that Americans were not to depend upon earthly kings or rulers but that our government was to be, as Lincoln would later say, "of the people, by the people, for the people."[1]

The Declaration of Independence was signed by fifty-six men who were known to be Congregationalist, Presbyterian, Anglican, Episcopal, Quaker, Unitarian, and Roman Catholic. Two were supposedly deists—Thomas Jefferson and Benjamin Franklin. All of them signed on to the principles of freedom. For the first time in human history, a nation was established on a solid foundation consistent with principles found in the Bible. Every one of our founders, with all of their distinctions and diversity, clearly understood that this nation was, in fact, established under God—not as a Christian nation, but as a nation whose founders clearly understood the basic principles necessary for free people to remain free. Despite doctrinal differences, they all knew a solid foundation when they saw it.

In my opinion, the church has been silent too often and the pulpits far too unprophetic to inspire repentance and the restoration of foundational principles. When I reference "common concerns," I am not inviting people to support a person or political party, but I am encouraging every person to find the principles necessary to live free as a believer, an individual, and a citizen of a free nation—and in this day there are few free nations. Let me touch on several areas that should deeply concern all of us:

First, *the ever-increasing size and control granted to the federal government by the voters and representatives in Washington is destroying any hope of real progress.* Our leaders protect the power of their positions by promising what only God and true charity can provide. Americans are being taught that they can depend on mankind rather than God. Politicians have become comfortable taking people's resources and disbursing them at will. We are not better for it; we are weaker because of it. I care deeply for the poor and helpless, but our nation's approach to the problem is making it worse. Voting for promises that sound compassionate is counterfeit charity. Only active involvement by caring people can produce positive progress.

Second, *the rapidly growing debt and the certain increase in taxes are bondage that will destroy any hope of future economic recovery and stability.* The job market will be more negatively impacted than one can possibly imagine. The ability for those who struggle to move forward will be drastically limited. If you want to alleviate suffering, practice charity, support meaningful outreaches, express compassion, provide for the needy, keep your job, and create opportunity while having protection and security, then you must get prayerfully involved and demand fiscal accountability and necessary adjustments. Without the restoration of sound economic principles, none of us will have the wherewithal to help anyone with their needs, because we will not be able to deal with our own. We cannot share what we do not have.

Third, *the lack of involvement on the part of Christians is diminishing our contribution to our country's well-being and, in fact, contributing to its downfall.* I have emphasized for many years the importance of Christians being inspired, informed, and involved. A great percentage of active church members, even in evangelical and Catholic churches, are not even registered to vote. Many who are registered never vote. Those who do vote are not always well informed. An uninformed electorate is potentially dangerous. They are easily manipulated. We need to understand the principles that made us great and those that must be preserved or restored.

Fourth, *the misinterpretation of founding principles is opening us up to great deception.* We must understand that rights come from God, not from mankind, government, or politicians. We have been granted God-given rights as our founders outlined in the Declaration of Independence: "We hold these truths to be self-evident, that all men are created equal, that they are endowed by their Creator with certain unalienable Rights, that among these are Life, Liberty and the pursuit of Happiness. That to secure these rights, Governments are instituted among Men."

These are God-given rights. Take note—only God can give life and give us true liberty that can be treasured and protected. But the founders said that we have the right to pursue happiness. We don't have a guarantee of happiness. We pursue those things that can bring success and happiness. Happiness is not something automatically given to people; it is something we must seek on our own. As Christians, we find real fullness in life by pursuing the source of life, living as free and responsible individuals, and pursuing the success and happiness that freedom affords us. We don't wait for someone to bring it to us. Freedom is God-given, and happiness depends upon the pursuit of it. Success isn't doled out. As the old saying goes, "A lot of people in America today are born on third base and think they hit a triple!"

People who have just received something and don't understand the responsibility that goes with both earning it and protecting it will prove to be unworthy and inadequate caretakers. This mentality is on the rise in our society, and only God can change it.

When our founders established this uniquely prosperous nation, they understood that freedom requires responsibility. This is not being communicated in our nation, and the church has failed to make it clear. Many professing Christians have participated in this terrible downward progression.

Fifth, *we have not embraced the value of human life.* How can the church not effectively address the tragedy of abortion? We must help people recognize the significance of life. The church is the most effective influence on earth working to strengthen the family and helping people understand the absolute value of human life.

Finally, *we have lost the importance of the family and marriage.* We are being pressed upon to condone as natural something that is in every way unnatural. Same-sex marriage is not only contrary to biblical truth, but it runs in direct opposition to nature.

It violates the first institution established by God—marriage between one man and one woman. It is also an assault on the picture of Christ coming for His bride, the church. It is an attack on the importance of this sacred relationship that leads to the fruitfulness of the marriage relationship with beautiful offspring and the families that are, in essence, the core strength in any community or society. Same-sex marriage may be legal, but it will never be beneficial.

It is the responsibility of the church to address these issues of national concern. Read the book of Nehemiah about how he led the people of Israel to restore the walls of Jerusalem. In the truest sense of the word, this is what I believe God is encouraging all of us as ministers and believers to begin doing in our nation. All of the Old Testament prophets warned Israel concerning the consequences of forsaking the moral boundaries God commanded them to keep in place as walls of protection.

It is the responsibility of the church to address these issues of national concern.

As Nehemiah built the walls and called the people to confess their sins, he reminded them of the cause of deterioration in the walls and the vulnerability of the people. In Nehemiah 9:16–17, he said, "Our ancestors were proud and stubborn, and they paid no attention to your commands. They refused to obey and did not remember the miracles you had done for them. Instead, they became stubborn and appointed a leader to take them back to their slavery in Egypt" (NLT). For many years our nation has chosen leaders to take us back into the bondage of this world.

As Christians, we are to love the people in the world but not be controlled by the ways of the world. We are not to be in bondage to the world's systems. Much of the population and the church live in bondage. Believers are not living in freedom that God offers. Unless the church begins to live in freedom and in the fullness of God's Spirit, we are not going to be able to help this nation rebuild the walls necessary to maintain the freedoms we have enjoyed.

We hear so often about the separation of church and state, interpreted to mean neither is to influence the other. Be assured, the state will influence you and the affairs of your life, your children, and generations beyond. I often hear Christians and church leaders excuse themselves from their civil responsibilities by referring to separation of church and state. This inappropriate response reveals a sad misunderstanding of the concept. The concept of separation of church and state is not in the Constitution. It is not in the Bill of Rights. It is a reference in a letter between Thomas Jefferson and some Baptist leaders in Danbury, Connecticut.[2] When Thomas Jefferson wrote about the "wall of separation between the church and state," the strong influence of preachers like Roger Williams led him to clearly understand that the wall is in place to protect the garden from the wilderness, not protect the wilderness from the gardens.[3] The garden of God—the influence of believers and people of faith—should always have a positive effect on the wilderness of government.

I encourage every believer to begin praying for leaders to be better informed, to speak out on issues of importance, and to begin participating as responsible citizens. I commit to seek, discover, and share the best sources of information possible. I am convinced that many pastors and church members also possess concern for our nation. Repentance, beginning on the part of the church, is where we start. We must recognize that we have failed to be rightly inspired, adequately informed, and totally involved. It is easy to answer, "Politics is a dirty business." But it is worse for us to sit back and mind our own business while someone else makes decisions that will lead us into the bondage our founders sought to escape. Whenever we have made the wrong decisions, our nation has often inappropriately adjusted. On other occasions, we have wisely corrected our course. As Christians, we must not engage in mockery or unfair accusations toward our enemies. We must present realistic, positive solutions and hope. It's not enough to curse the darkness; we must shine the light.

I fully believe that if the church becomes prayerfully involved in the political process, then we can see this nation turn back to the light and glory of liberating truth.

Chapter 39

BOLD WITNESSES

F reedom's future rests on the shoulders of bold people who will not be silent about truth and the absolute principles upon which it stands. As a Christian, I believe the future of our freedom depends upon true believers waking up and standing up like New Testament Christians. In the early church, Christians were ready and willing to die for what they had experienced and believed. Today it is difficult to get those who profess to know Christ to be serious about living for Him, much less dying for what they claim to believe. Why can't almost 250 million Americans who claim to believe in God, the Bible, and Jesus Christ as the Savior[1] have as much influence as the very small, identifiable groups of bold activists impacting our national direction and culture?

Life, liberty, and the ability to pursue happiness will continue to rapidly diminish if Christians do not become bold witnesses. Paul said, "It is already the hour to awaken from sleep . . . and put on the armor of light" (Romans 13:11–12). May I call your attention to the kind of witnesses necessary if we are to see America and the world impacted by God's transforming power? It is clearly revealed and demonstrated through the lives of New Testament believers in Acts 3 and 4.

In chapter 3, Peter and John were instrumental in releasing a miraculous demonstration of God's power to heal. Even the unbelieving public called it a notable miracle. When they were questioned and challenged by some observers, these bold witnesses proclaimed that it was the power in the name of Jesus. Peter then called all to repentance, telling them that Jesus is the One God sent to forgive, restore, and bless those who would believe and turn from their sins. Can you believe what happened next? Smug, lifeless, religious people, priests, and leaders rose up to silence them. Then with critical animosity, they asked, "By what power, or in what name, have you done this?" (Acts 4:7). In other words, how did you release this obvious miracle power?

The Bible says, "Peter, filled with the Holy Spirit" (v. 8)—the only way any Christians will ever have the love, courage and power to be a bold witness—said to them, "by the name of Jesus Christ the Nazarene, whom you crucified, whom God raised from the dead" that this miracle occurred (v. 10). He declared that this very Christ must be the cornerstone upon which you build a secure future. All personal and national freedom must be established and built on this solid Rock, God's unshakable foundation of truth.

Without hesitancy or reservation, Peter boldly continued, "There is salvation in no one else; for there is no other name under heaven that has been given among men by which we must be saved" (v. 12). The crowd saw the obvious confidence in Peter and John and marveled because they recognized that they had been with Jesus. But then, just as in our day, the powers that be—political, religious, prevailing ideologies, and the Council—commanded them not to speak or teach in the name of Jesus. In other words, to put it bluntly, "Shut up. Get back undercover or whatever rock you came out from under. Get out of sight." Then in verses 19–20, "Peter and John answered and said to them, 'Whether it is right in the sight of God to give heed to you rather than to God, you be the judge; for we cannot stop speaking about what we have *seen* and *heard.*'"

It seems many who go to church are at best content to soak up what they hear or observe and consider truth, but never release that river of life throughout their own communities and unto the ends of the earth. Could it be that they have heard too little and have seen too little of spiritual and supernatural significance to be willing to share it at all, much less with excitement and boldly in power?

The answer to our problems and how to address the challenges we face is given in the following verses. The unbelievers raged, and the people devised futile things, and "the rulers were gathered together against the Lord and against His Christ" (Acts 4:26). Then Peter said, "Now, Lord, take note of their threats, and grant that Your bond-servants may speak Your word with all confidence, while You extend Your hand to heal, and signs and wonders take place through the name of Your holy servant Jesus" (vv. 29–30).

The key verse, the absolutely essential power necessary to become bold witnesses, is found in Acts 4:31: "And when they had prayed, the place where they had gathered together was shaken, and they were all filled with the Holy Spirit and began to speak the word of God with boldness." If we are going to see a positive impact made on our personal, local, and national lives because of the effect of bold witnesses, it will be because we have experienced this same power.

God, let it happen in our lives, in the church, in our nation, and to the ends of the earth!

Chapter 40

ANSWERING JESUS'S PRAYER

M any times I have said to friends and viewers of *LIFE Today*, "If you want your prayers answered, seek to be an answer to someone else's prayer!" As Betty and I have supported missions and ministry endeavors all over the world, we have seen the things we were able to do come as a direct answer to someone's prayer, not just a need met. When we give attention to the concerns of our Father and hear the heart cry of others, there is no question that God grants us light in our darkest moments and we become a fruitful garden, truly an ever-flowing stream.

My personal focus now and for the rest of my life is to see Jesus's prayer for us in John 17 fulfilled in our day. Our Lord expressed excitement to His Father about the glory that had been revealed through Him to His followers now being revealed to the world through them. He desires that we each become one with the Father as He (Jesus) is. We are to capture the heart of the Father because we have been totally captivated by His heart. His will becomes our will, His concerns our concerns, and His focus our focus. As we submit to Him, presenting ourselves as living sacrifices, we will be transformed by the renewing of our minds to know what the good, acceptable and perfect will of God is (Romans 12:1–2).

Jesus prayed for us to be protected from the evil one and to become holy, consecrated by the truth of His Word. Paul referred to this process as "the washing of water with the word" (Ephesians 5:26). Jesus taught that abiding in Him enables us to know the truth that sets us free. It is critically important—absolutely necessary—for us to come into this oneness with the Father in order for the other prayerful requests of our Savior to be fulfilled.

Consider the part of Jesus's prayer that we be one with the Father as He is (John 17:22). Think about that a moment. Jesus was continually seeking to do only those things that please the Father. He moved as God directed His steps. He would separate Himself from the sounds of the world to know clearly the Father's mind and be able to live in sync with His heart.

When we look at how divided the family of God is, we also need to consider the illustration Jesus shared concerning the father in the story of the prodigal son. This boy took from his father money that he had not earned or helped produce. He left the father's presence, moved out of his shelter, and wasted everything the father had provided and entrusted to him. He damaged the family's reputation with no regard for it, squandered his wealth in riotous living, and found himself in want. He was in such desperate need that of all things, this Jewish son had to live in a pigpen

feeding unclean animals and eating what they ate. This was the lowest place a Jewish person could sink, because their laws and customs forbade contact with pigs.

What was the response of the father concerning his son's rebellion? He certainly didn't condone it. He didn't approve of it or continue to enable it. He didn't act as the federal government often does by funding his rebellion in order to make him more comfortable. He prayed continually for the son. He cared deeply for him. The father's love never diminished and he looked with a longing in his heart every day for that boy to return to the shelter, shadow, and security of the father's house. Sure enough, the day came, and he rejoiced to see his son come home! In love he embraced him, covered him, and confirmed his sonship.

This should be the attitude of every Christian toward other believers even when they are defeated by sin. While not approving their actions, we continually pray for and long for a repentant heart leading to a return to the watch care of the Shepherd. In order for us to be perfected in the unity Jesus prayed for, we must have the love of the Father for one another. This is absolutely crucial.

This last area of concern Jesus prayed for His followers is perhaps what seems to many as the impossible dream—"that they may be perfected in unity" (v. 23). Knowing what I know about myself, other Christians, and especially ministers, this is the most difficult to see answered. If Jesus prayed it, however, it is more important than words alone can describe and obviously will be continually assaulted by the powers and principalities of darkness. The thought of believers being perfected in unity and

love—truly becoming a family of faith with hearts in harmony with our Father in heaven—causes the forces of hell to tremble. The church standing on this foundation will overpower the realm of darkness, deception, and destruction, setting free all captives who respond to the kingdom reality Jesus prayed for.

As a teenager reading the biography of D. L. Moody, I was highly influenced by a statement Moody's friend Henry Varley made to the young evangelist: "The world has yet to see what God can do with a man fully consecrated to Him."[1] As a boy, I said, "I want to be that person." I still do! But even more, I want the world to see what God can do with a people who truly become disciples—His church on this earth, totally surrendered and committed to becoming an answer to Jesus's prayers.

Would you join me seeking to be one with the Father, perfected in unity so the world will know we are His disciples because of our love for Him, for one another, and for a world in darkness and pain?

During the past twenty years, God has led me to meet with many diverse Christian leaders, which religious tradition and the opinions of others had taught me to avoid. During these times of sharing and seeking together to know God's heart, I have never disregarded or knowingly compromised God's Word—and I never will. As a result, I have experienced firsthand the powerful truth of the psalmist, "How good and pleasant it is for brothers to dwell together in unity" (Psalm 133:1). During these exchanges, I have many times felt what I perceived

as the Father's pleasure just as Betty and I experienced it when we watched our three children playing together in joyful harmony.

Would you join me seeking to be one with the Father, perfected in unity so the world will know we are His disciples because of our love for Him, for one another, and for a world in darkness and pain? I may not know you personally, but I love you and I ask you to join with me seeking to be an answer to Jesus's prayers so that the world may behold the glory of the Father and the Son in our lives!

Conclusion

AMERICA'S ONLY HOPE

The hope for America is the hope for freedom and the only true hope for the world. It is the transforming power of gospel truth demonstrated by changed lives and delivered by Spirit-filled believers.

The New Testament church—His church—is made up of blood-bought, born-again, baptized-into-Christ people who have a personal relationship with Jesus as Lord and know Creator God as Father. This is our Lord's body left here on earth and charged with the Great Commission to make disciples of Christ—not to make church folks or mere church members or religious clones void of Jesus's life, love, and Spirit.

The uniquely designed individual members of the body of Christ must now come together in supernatural unity submitted to the Head—Jesus. The members and parts can be found on every continent, in every nation, in various sectarian groups and denominations around the world. Many in various groups have truly been born again into His church and have miraculously come to know Him in a personal relationship. They recognized the Shepherd's voice when they heard it, and they responded and followed because they are His sheep.

The Lord who is our Shepherd will miraculously calm raging storms within our lives and around us, leading us beside waters made still and calm by His abiding presence and into green pastures, even turning barren land into fertile fields of opportunity. He will comfort all in the shadow of any valley, including the valley of death. He will do what no earthly power or new substitute for Pharaoh, a dictator, monarchy, president, or Congress could ever adequately accomplish. Jesus, our Lord, will prepare a table for us, providing for us even in the presence of all enemies, skeptics, doubters, and accusers. Goodness, mercy, and grace, as well as His provision, will follow us all the days of our life. We fear no evil, horrible though it may be, for the Lord is with us, guiding us to security as we stand against the fierce flood and intentions of evil. Wisdom will direct our steps, and the hedge of His Word will protect us. The gates of hell shall not prevail!

As my friend Rev. Samuel Rodriguez says, our nation's hope does not ride on the agenda of a donkey or elephant, but rather the Lamb. Consider his exhortation in what he calls "The Lamb's Agenda."[1]

According to Rev. Rodriguez, the Lamb's agenda activates a kingdom culture firewall of righteousness and justice. In other words, in order to defend life and protect liberty and facilitate the platform by which all Americans can pursue happiness, we must apply biblical optics and apply corrective lenses to spiritual and cultural myopia. In other words, if I am following the Lamb's agenda, when I wake up in the morning, I don't see a Hispanic, black, white, or Asian. I don't see a denomination or a theological distinction. I am first and foremost a child of the living God! I am a born-again Christian! I am a child of God! I am a follower of Jesus. I am a Christian—first and foremost! I am a believer, and my vertical identity empowers my horizontal reality. And when we vote, we must vote our vertical reality.

In a clarion call to believers around the world, Rev. Rodriguez addresses those "giants" of perversion, mockery, oppression, destruction, and every other evil in society:

> So to every narrative and spirit that facilitates the platform of moral relativism, of spiritual apathy, of cultural decadence and ecclesiastical lukewarmness, we say the following: For every Pharaoh there must be a Moses. For every Goliath there must be a David. For every Nebuchadnezzar there must be a Daniel. For every Jezebel there must be an Elijah. For every Herod there must be a Jesus. And for every devil that rises up against you there is a mightier God who will rise up for you![2]

As His people called by His name come together in brokenness and humility, turning from all of our indifference and wicked ways, our Lord Almighty Creator will hear from heaven and will forgive us, cover us, and heal the people and our land (2 Chronicles 7:14). That is God's promise, and it is greater than any promise a politician, candidate, or government may claim to provide.

It is time for the American government to once again be on His shoulders as we—His ambassadors, the church—assume the responsibility God has given us to lead and make a *salt* and *light* impact on this earth. Salt protects and preserves the precious. Light exposes the error of our ways and reveals the necessary corrections that must be made.

Just as the dry bones responded to His Word by coming together in supernatural unity and the Spirit filled those bones, raising them up to become a mighty army (Ezekiel 37:1–14), so shall the church in this day become the mighty army of God and faithful witnesses He has commissioned us to be, and our nation will be restored. This is our hope!

ACKNOWLEDGMENTS

For Betty, my beautiful bride of over fifty years. Next to Jesus you are without a doubt my greatest source of inspiration and support. Your visible concern and prayers for our nation moved me to action by writing and speaking to remind everyone of freedom's blessings, the truth that birthed it, and what is necessary to protect and preserve it. Thank you for always standing with me and encouraging me. You are a delight.

For our son Randy, who edited and organized the content of this book. I couldn't have done it without you. Thank you for sharing insight and important corrections over the years as I attempted to share the wisdom that comes from above. I am proud of you and your family. You are a great husband and father.

For our precious daughter Robin, now in the presence of our Lord Jesus in heaven. For forty years you brought indescribable joy to all who knew you. Your story is one of a life well lived as a witness for Christ and the abundant life He freely offers. You sowed seeds of life every day on your journey on this earth, and we now witness the beautiful fruit of it in the lives of your children and everyone you touched as you demonstrated the transforming power of the gospel.

For Rhonda, our first child. Throughout your life you have continually inspired all of us with your passionate pursuit of the Father's heart and your determination to please God above all and to be a devoted wife to your husband and mother to your awesome children. And now as the grandmother of our great-grandson, you are enjoying your children and family as much as anyone on this planet—and what a joy it is for us to watch! Mom and I are so proud of you.

In addition to my family, I would like to thank all the tributaries of life, love, and wisdom who have poured their knowledge, insight, and inspiration into my life for the sake of freedom and God's kingdom purpose on earth through His family—the church. I thank you and bless you as we seek to honor our heavenly Father together by blessing those He gave His Son to redeem and set free so they can totally reveal the Father in all of His grace and glory.

NOTES

Introduction: Not Too Late to Turn the Tide
1. U.S. Information Agency, "Benjamin Franklin's Rising Sun," in *An Outline of American Government*, republished on the website American History: From Revolution to Reconstruction and Beyond, http://www.let.rug.nl/usa/outlines/government-1991 /topics/benjamin-franklins-rising-sun.php.

Chapter 1: A Nation Gone Mad
1. James Madison, First Inaugural Address, March 4, 1809, Library of Congress American Memory website, Journal of the Senate of the United States of America, 1789–1873, vol. 4: 367, https://memory.loc.gov/cgi-bin/query/r?ammem/hlaw:@field%28DOCID+@ lit%28sj004410%29%29.

Chapter 2: Mobocracy in the Heartland
1. All quotes from Abraham Lincoln in this chapter come from his Lyceum Address, January 27, 1838, available at Abraham Lincoln Online, http://www.abrahamlincolnonline.org/lincoln /speeches/lyceum.htm.

Chapter 3: Most People
1. Gary Langer, "Poll: Most Americans Say They're Christians," ABC News, July 18, 2015, http://abcnews.go.com/US/story?id=90356.

Chapter 5: Bottom-Up, Inside-Out: Internal Change First
1. Adam Smith, *The Wealth of Nations*, book IV, chapter II, p. 456, para. 9, quoted in "Adam Smith Quotes," Adam Smith Institute, http://www.adamsmith.org/adam-smith-quotes/.

Chapter 6: Hope and Change
1. Edward Everett Hale, "Lend a Hand," in James Dalton Morrison, ed., *Masterpieces of Religious Verse* (New York. Harper, 1948).

Chapter 7: The Importance of Gratitude
1. Rutherford B. Hayes, "Proclamation 247—Thanksgiving Day, 1880," November 1, 1880, The American Presidency Project, http://www.presidency.ucsb.edu/ws/?pid=68555.

Chapter 8: Return to Wisdom
1. Lewis R. Harley, *The Life of Charles Thomson* (Philadelphia: G.W. Jacob, 1900).

Chapter 9: Kissing Freedom Good-bye
1. Ronald Reagan, "Encroaching Control" (address to the annual meeting of the Phoenix Chamber of Commerce, March 30, 1961).

Chapter 11: Freedom Must Be Protected
1. Benjamin Franklin, quoted in the notes of Dr. James McHenry, first published in *The American Historical Review*, vol. 11 (1906), 618, quoted online at Bartleby.com, http://www.bartleby .com/73/1593.html.

Chapter 12: The Restoration of Freedom
1. National Park Service, ParkNet, "Determining the Facts: Reading 2: Francis Scott Key and the Writing of 'The Star-Spangled Banner,'" http://www.nps.gov/nr/twhp/wwwlps/lessons /137fomc/137facts2.htm.

2. Lynch v. Donnelly, 465 U.S. 668 (1984).

3. Edmund Burke, *Reflections on the Revolution of France*, 1790, http://www.ourcivilisation.com
/burke/index.htm.

Part Four: Evil Must Be Fought

1. Martin Luther King Jr., *Stride Toward Freedom: The Montgomery Story* (New York: Harper and
Brothers, 1984), 51.

Chapter 13: The Face of Evil

1. Anthony Joseph et al., "'He Walked Out of a Building, Got in the Car . . . We Took the Shot':
US Military Chiefs Reveal How Jihadi John Was 'Evaporated' in the Street in Midnight Drone
Strike," *Daily Mail*, November 12, 2015, updated November 13, 2015, http://www.dailymail
.co.uk/news/article-3316497/Has-Jihadi-John-killed-drone-strike-Officials-claim-British
-ISIS-fanatic-targeted-Raqqa.html.

2. Douglas Harper, *Dictionary.com Online Etymology Dictionary*, s.v. "bewildered," http://
dictionary.reference.com/browse/bewildered.

3. George Washington Carver, letter to YMCA official Jack Boyd in Denver, Colorado, March 1,
1927.

Chapter 14: Confronting Evil

1. Pew Research Center, "US Public Becoming Less Religious," November 3, 2015, http://www
.pewforum.org/2015/11/03/u-s-public-becoming-less-religious/.

2. Ronald Reagan, "Tear Down This Wall" (speech, West Berlin, June 12, 1987).

3. Life Matters, "Number of Abortions—Abortion Counters," http://www.numberofabortions.com.

4. Conor Friedersdorf, "Why Dr. Kermit Gossnell's Trial Should Be a Front-Page Story," *The
Atlantic*, April 12, 2013, http://www.theatlantic.com/national/archive/2013/04/why-dr
-kermit-gosnells-trial-should-be-a-front-page-story/274944/.

5. Abraham Lincoln, First Inaugural Address, March 4, 1861, Library of Congress American
Memory website, "The Abraham Lincoln Papers at the Library of Congress," http://memory
.loc.gov/cgi-bin/query/r?ammem/mal:@field%28DOCID+@lit%28d0773800%29%29.

Chapter 15: Subtle Evils

1. Calvin Coolidge, Vice-Presidential Acceptance Address, Northampton, Massachusetts, July 27,
1920.

Chapter 17: Know Justice, Know Peace

1. George Washington, "Circular to States on Farewell to the Army," June 8, 1783, http://memory
.loc.gov/cgi-bin/ampage?collId=mgw4&fileName=gwpage092.db&recNum=161.

2. John Adams, Inaugural Address, March 4, 1797, Yale Law School Avalon Project, http://avalon
.law.yale.edu/18th_century/adams.asp.

3. Abraham Lincoln, Second Inaugural Address, March 4, 1865, Library of Congress American
Memory website, "The Abraham Lincoln Papers at the Library of Congress," https://memory.
loc.gov/cgi-bin/query/r?ammem/mal:@field%28DOCID+@lit%28d4361300%29%29.

Chapter 21: America and the Poor

1. Ben Carson, *Gifted Hands: The Ben Carson Story* (Grand Rapids: Zondervan, 2011).

Chapter 22: Thou Shalt Not Covet

1. Robert Rector and Rachel Sheffield, "Understanding Poverty in the United States: Surprising
Facts about America's Poor," The Heritage Foundation, September 13, 2011, http://www.
heritage.org/research/reports/2011/09/understanding-poverty-in-the-united-states
-surprising-facts-about-americas-poor.

Chapter 23: Jesus Started with Inequality

1. Mark Trumbull, "Is Income Inequality as Bad as Obama Says? In Many Ways, Yes," *Christian Science Monitor*, January 7, 2014, http://www.csmonitor.com/USA/Politics/DC-Decoder/2014/0107/Is-income-inequality-as-bad-as-Obama-says-In-many-ways-yes.-video.
2. Jim Wallis, "God Hates Inequality," Huffington Post, May 25, 2011, http://www.huffingtonpost.com/jim-wallis/god-hates-inequality_b_40170.html.
3. Elise Amyx with Jay Richards, "What's Wrong with Inequality?" TownHall.com, January 18, 2014, http://townhall.com/columnists/eliseamyx/2014/01/18/whats-wrong-with-inequality-n1780872/page/full.

Chapter 24: Don't Kill the Goose

1. Aesop for Children, "The Goose and the Golden Egg," 1919, http://mythfolklore.net/aesopica/milowinter/80.htm.

Chapter 25: America's New Pharaoh

1. White House Office of the Press Secretary, "News Conference by the President," news release, January 14, 2013, https://www.whitehouse.gov/the-press-office/2013/01/14/news-conference-president.

Chapter 26: Small God, Big Government

1. James Madison, "The Structure of the Government Must Furnish the Proper Checks and Balances between the Different Departments," *The Federalist* no. 51, first published in *Independent Journal*, February 6, 1788, Constitution Society, http://www.constitution.org/fed/federa51.htm.

Chapter 27: The Church of State

1. Kevin Miller, *Freedom Nationally, Virtue Locally—or Socialism* (Greenwood Village, CO: MT6 Media, 2010).

Chapter 28: What, Not Who

1. Craig Vincent Mitchell, PhD, "The Gospel of Jesus Christ Versus the Gospel of Big Government," *Justice and Righteousness* (blog), *Christian Post*, November 3, 2013, http://blogs.christianpost.com/justice-and-righteousness/the-gospel-of-jesus-christ-vs-the-gospel-of-biggovernment-18625/.
2. Ronald Reagan, "Election Eve Address: A Vision for America," November 3, 1980 , Ronald Reagan Presidential Library and Museum, "Ronald Reagan's Major Speeches, 1964–89," https://reaganlibrary.archives.gov/archives/reference/11.3.80.html.

Part Eight: Every Life Matters

1. CNN Democratic Presidential Debate, October 13, 2015, http://cnnpressroom.blogs.cnn.com/2015/10/13/cnn-democratic-debate-full-transcript/.

Chapter 29: Equal Value and Dignity

1. Charles Merriam, "Recent Tendencies," *A History of American Political Theories* (1903), chapter 8, "First Principles Series," Heritage Foundation, http://www.heritage.org/initiatives/first-principles/primary-sources/charles-merriam-explains-progressive-political-science.
2. Lyndon Johnson, "To Fulfill These Rights" (commencement address, Howard University, June 4, 1965), LBJ Presidential Library, http://www.lbjlib.utexas.edu/johnson/archives.hom/speeches.hom/650604.asp.

NOTES

Chapter 31: Celebration of Life
1. Frank Newport, "Three Quarters of Americans Identify as Christians," Gallup, December 24, 2014, http://www.gallup.com/poll/180347/three-quarters-americans-identify-christian.aspx.

Chapter 32: The Precious Is Trampled
1. Dr. Ben Carson, interview by the author, *LIFE Today*, September 9, 2014.
2. Matthew 5:13–14; alluded to in Ronald Reagan's "Election Eve Address: A Vision for America," November 3, 1980.

Part Nine: Families Are the Foundation of Society
1. Jim Garlow, "Christian Leaders: The Chamberlains and the Churchills," WND, June 23, 2015, http://www.wnd.com/2015/06/christian-leaders-the-chamberlains-and-the-churchills/.

Chapter 35: A Fatherless Nation
1. Obergefell v. Hodges, 576 U.S. ___ (2015).
2. Cheryl Clarke and Monica Bey-Clarke, *Keesha and Her Two Moms Go Swimming* (Dodi Press, 2011).

Chapter 38: Common Concerns of the Church and State
1. Abraham Lincoln, "Gettysburg Address," (address delivered at dedication of soldiers' cemetery, Gettysburg, Pennsylvania, November 19, 1963), Abraham Lincoln Online, http://www.abrahamlincolnonline.org/lincoln/speeches/gettysburg.htm.
2. Thomas Jefferson, January 1, 1802, letter to Danbury Baptist Association, as quoted in Albert E. Bergh, ed., *The Writings of Thomas Jefferson*, vol. XVI (Washington, DC: The Thomas Jefferson Memorial Association of the United States, 1904), 281–82, https://www.tgm.org/SeparationLetters.html.
3. Roger Williams, "Mr. Cotton's Letter Lately Printed, Examined and Answered," *The Complete Writings of Roger Williams*, vol. 1 (New York: Russell & Russell, 1963), 108.

Chapter 39: Bold Witnesses
1. Pew Research Center, Forum on Religion and Public Life, "Global Christianity—A Report on the Size and Distribution of the World's Christian Population," December 19, 2011, http://www.pewforum.org/2011/12/19/global-christianity-exec/.

Chapter 40: Answering Jesus's Prayer
1. Mark Facklet, "The World Has Yet to See . . . ," *Christianity Today* 25 (1990), http://www.christianitytoday.com/history/issues/issue-25/world-has-yet-to-see.html

Conclusion: America's Only Hope
1. Samuel Rodriguez, *The Lamb's Agenda* (Nashville: Thomas Nelson, 2013).
2. Ibid., 20–21.

ABOUT THE AUTHOR

James Robison is the founder and president of LIFE Outreach International, and the founder and publisher of The Stream (stream.org). Since 1968, James has presented the gospel on television. He launched the daily television program *LIFE Today* with his wife, Betty, in 1995. James has preached in over six hundred citywide evangelistic crusades attended by more than twenty million people and personally inspired religious, political, and social leaders across five decades.

IF YOU ENJOYED THIS BOOK, WILL YOU CONSIDER SHARING THE MESSAGE WITH OTHERS?

Mention the book in a blog post or through Facebook, Twitter, Pinterest, or upload a picture through Instagram.

Recommend this book to those in your small group, book club, workplace, and classes.

Head over to facebook.com/worthypublishing, "LIKE" the page, and post a comment as to what you enjoyed the most.

Tweet "I recommend reading #TheStream by @revjamesrobison // @worthypub"

Pick up a copy for someone you know who would be challenged and encouraged by this message.

Write a book review online.

Visit us at worthypublishing.com

twitter.com/worthypub

worthypub.tumblr.com

facebook.com/worthypublishing

pinterest.com/worthypub

instagram.com/worthypub

youtube.com/worthypublishing